iPhone 13 User Gu Seniors

Tips And Tricks For Beginners And Seniors In Troubleshooting Apple iPhone 13 To Become A Pro User

Willie Anne Candy

Table of Contents

Introduction

The iPhone 13 series includes the iPhone 13, iPhone 13 Mini, iPhone 13 Pro, and iPhone 13 Pro Max. The device is power-driven by the latest A15 Bionic Processor, which guarantees fast processing speed and a high refresh rate. Like the previous iPhone models, it also features a triple-lens camera and a front camera, which comes with 12 megapixels. In this new device, Face ID is one of the leading sensors, alongside ultra-broadband, gyro, accelerometer, barometer, compass, and others. Going further, the device features a 6.7-inch super retina display, which makes for a brighter and lengthy screen. Alongside its display features, the new device also features some camera improvements and features, such as being able to record video in ProRes, shooting cinematic video, shooting or capturing macro videos and photos, and so much more. Most importantly, this new device runs on iOS 15, a new operating system released by Apple that also has its own features. Connectivity and browsing won't be an issue with the new iPhone 13 series because it comes with 5G connectivity, 5.0 Bluetooth compatibility, and the new Wi-Fi 6.

The iPhone 13 is a very complex device with many features and can be challenging to master. Many iPhone owners can feel overwhelmed at first by their new gadget and are at a loss for where to start. This book puts together an easy-to-follow guide for beginners and seniors who want to become advanced iPhone 13 users. Also, you will learn all the tips and tricks for your Apple iPhone 13 and customize it to work the way you want.

Elderly people may not use their smartphones as proficiently as compared to their grandkids, if helped and followed step-by-step, they can quickly learn all the necessary iPhone functionality. This comprehensive manual will assist you in getting started with the iPhone 13 and discovering all of its wonderful capabilities. Learn how to tweak the settings of your iPhone 13 series to make it operate exactly how you want it to, if not better.

In order to utilize the best features of the iPhone 13, it is important to understand some of the basics. By learning how to configure your phone properly, you'll increase the odds of using it in the best possible way. Whether you need to set up your email or use the GPS features of your iPhone, this guide can help you get the most out of your device.

Chapter 1

The iPhone 13 and iPhone 13 mini are two new iPhone models.

The iPhone 13 and iPhone 13 mini, which were released on September 14, 2021, are Apple's newest flagship iPhones at a lower price point and are available alongside the more costly iPhone 13 Pro and iPhone 13 Pro Max. The iPhone 13 and iPhone 13 mini are perfect for consumers who don't require professional-grade photography capabilities.

The iPhone 13 mini, with a screen size of 5.4 inches, is the successor to the iPhone 12 mini, while the iPhone 13, with a screen size of 6.1 inches, is the replacement for the iPhone 12. Flat corners, an aerospace-grade aluminum enclosure, a glass back, and a little increase in thickness characterize both of the new iPhone 13 models, which are almost identical in design to the iPhone 12 variants (7.65mm). Pink, Blue, Midnight (black), Starlight (silver/gold), (PRODUCT) RED and Green are the colors offered for the iPhone 13 models.

Both of the most recent models have Super Retina XDR displays that are 28 percent brighter. The iPhone 13 mini has a resolution of 2340x1080 at 476 pixels per inch, whereas the iPhone 13 has a resolution of 2532x1170 at 460 pixels per inch. iPhones with HDR have a maximum brightness of 1200 nits. They also have True Tone, Wide Color, and Haptic Touch for feedback.

The True-Depth camera technology on the front has been improved, and the Face ID notch has been reduced in size, taking up less total area. The iPhone 13 and 13 mini, like last year's models, include a Ceramic Shield cover glass that is embedded with nano-ceramic crystals for greater drop protection. The new iPhones have IP68 water and dust resistance, and they can be submerged in 6 meters of water for up to 30 minutes. They can also be exposed to dust for a long time.

The latest iPhones are powered by an improved A15 Bionic chip. It has a 6-core CPU with 2 performance cores and 4 efficiency cores, as well as a 4-core GPU (one GPU core less than the Pro variants) and a 16-core Neural Engine.

A new diagonal dual-lens back camera with 12 megapixel wide and ultra-wide sensors has been added to the mix. The wide camera has a new f/1.6 aperture that lets in 47% more light, as well as Sensor-Shift Stabilization, while the ultra-wide camera has a new f/2.4 aperture for better low-light performance.

The iPhone 13 models gain Cinematic Mode, a feature that uses rack focus to seamlessly shift focus from one subject to another, artfully blurring the background and creating movie-quality depth effects, in addition to the standard Portrait Mode, Night Mode, Time-Lapse, and other photographic capabilities. The depth of field and blur can be changed using the iPhone's camera app in Cinematic mode, which shoots in Dolby HDR. The iPhone 13 models can also record 4K video at up to 60 frames per second.

Deep Fusion, a carryover from iPhone 12, activates in mid-to-low-light scenarios to bring out texture and detail, and Smart HDR 4 identifies up to four people in a photo and optimizes the contrast, lighting, and skin tones for each of them.

Photographic Styles are an improved type of filter that selectively mutes or boosts the vibrancy of an image without affecting skin tones. There are options for vibrant, rich contrast, warm, and cool, as well as tone and warmth settings for customization and refinement.

The Face ID facial recognition system on Apple's iPhone 13 and 13 mini works with the 12-megapixel front-facing camera, which supports Smart HDR 4, Deep Fusion, Night Mode, Cinematic Mode, Night Mode Selfies, and more.

Although 5G connectivity is included for smoother video streaming, higher-definition FaceTime chats, and improved gaming, the ultra-fast mmWave speeds are once again limited to major US cities. Slower sub-6GHz 5G speeds are already available in more rural parts of the United States and other countries, and more 5G bands are being used to spread the coverage of 5G across more places.

The iPhone 13 and 13 mini have a U1 Ultra Wideband processor for spatial awareness, as well as Wi-Fi 6 and Bluetooth 5.0.

When 5G isn't accessible, Gigabit LTE is enabled, and a Smart Data Mode reverts to an LTE connection when 5G speeds aren't required to save battery life. The new iPhone 13 models allow dual eSIM and don't come with a physical SIM by default, although a nano-SIM slot is still available.

Larger batteries and the more efficient A15 chip have greatly enhanced battery life. The iPhone 13 mini has a battery life of up to 1.5 hours longer than the iPhone 12 mini, and the iPhone 13 has a battery life of up to 2.5 hours longer than the iPhone 12.

Storage capacity ranges from 128GB to 512GB on the top end. A three-axis gyro, an accelerometer, proximity sensor, ambient light sensor, and barometer are all built-in.

The iPhone 13 and iPhone 13 mini contain built-in magnets and are compatible with MagSafe accessories, charging at up to 15W with Apple's MagSafe Charger, just like last year's iPhones (2020). The iPhones also support fast charging, which allows for a 50 percent charge in 30 minutes when using a 20W power adapter.

The iPhone 13 and 13 mini do not come with a power adaptor or EarPods, and these items must be purchased separately. They do come with a charging cable that converts USB-C to Lightning.

Pricing and Availability

The iPhone 13 mini starts at $699, while the iPhone 13 starts at $799, with no price hikes in 2021. Preorders for the iPhone 13 variants began on September 17, 2021, with the first units shipping on September 24, 2021. Apple's web shop, Apple retail stores, carriers, and third-party retail stores all sell the iPhone 13 versions.

Reviews

The iPhone 13 has received generally excellent reviews, mainly for improvements in battery life, the speedier A15 chip, and camera tweaks, although some have criticized it as being an iterative update that lacks enough new features to justify upgrading from an iPhone 12.

Battery life this year is "outstanding," according to Dieter Bohn of The Verge, citing real-world tests. While the smaller iPhone 13 mini has improved, Engadget notes that it is still "shorter than the usual smartphone."

"Details are sharp and accurate, colors are rich without being oversaturated, focusing is fast and reliable, portrait mode is good enough to use on a daily basis, and low light and night vision are both exceptional," Bohn remarked of the camera. According to Joanna Stern of the Wall Street Journal, while the iPhone 13's camera enhancements are welcome, they aren't enough to persuade an iPhone 12 owner to switch.

According to CNET, the iPhone 13's performance and battery life are great, and it will be a good choice for most people.

The iPhone 13 is the phone for those who don't need a certain function. It's in the middle of the mini and max sizes, with just enough features to make it valuable. The more expensive pro version is for those who want a better display or more camera features.

With only a modest thickness increase, a diagonal camera layout, and a smaller notch, the design didn't vary significantly year over year. MagSafe charging is still available, and the base capacity has been upgraded from 64GB to 128GB for the same price.

Due to the changes, we believe this release would have been referred to as 12S rather than 13 in Apple's original "S" naming scheme. Apple usually only makes camera and battery life enhancements for "S" years, which is primarily what we see here.

The company's decision to reduce the notch appears to be a double-edged sword. On the one hand, the notch is smaller, and the system's technology has shrunk to fit it. Apple, on the other hand, has done nothing with the increased space.

Customers who are unfamiliar with the iPhone will consider the notch to be unsightly when compared to the competition. Samsung and others have switched to hole-punch cameras, which allow for eye-catching edge-to-edge screens, but Apple is stuck with its "old" notch design. The notch is still there to house the True Depth camera array that powers the secure Face ID system, but that won't make the average user feel better.

Although the A15 Bionic is more powerful, most users will not notice the difference. The overhead offered by the powerful chip, on the other hand, will give room for rapid iPhone operation for many years to come. The improved battery life metric is mostly due to the processor's higher efficiency.

Photographic Styles and Cinematic Mode are sure to impress a lot of new consumers, but it's unclear how frequently they'll be used in ordinary life. Despite its early faults, we like Cinematic Mode and believe it will continue to improve with time.

We believe that anyone upgrading from an iPhone older than the iPhone 12 series will be blown away by the improved battery life and camera. Although the year-over-year boost is more difficult to sell, there is enough here for some to warrant it. Regardless, Apple has again had another successful smartphone, and we believe the iPhone 13 will be the most popular model in 2021.

Advantages:

- Doubled storage capacity

- The A15 Bionic chip still has significant performance improvements.

- The battery life has improved.

- The notch is a little smaller.

- Photographic Styles are a fantastic new camera function.

- There's a lot of promise in Cinematic Mode.

- MagSafe has never been more handy.

- The design is still sleek, but the colors have been updated.

- Two eSIM cards are supported.

Disadvantages

- Camera upgrades are minimal.

- Cases from the previous generation will not fit.

- Performance improvements aren't as dramatic as in previous years.

- 6E has no WiFi.

- The price of the iPhone 12 has gone up.

Design

With the iPhone 12, Apple ditched the rounded sides that had been utilized on iPhones since the iPhone 6, opting instead for a flat-sided design with squared-off corners, similar to the iPhone 4 and 5 and matching the iPad Pro.

The whole iPhone 13 lineup has the same flat-edged design, and the iPhone 13 models have roughly the identical body design as the iPhone 12 models they replace. There's an all-glass front and a colorful all-glass rear, both of which are held together by a color-matched aluminum frame.

The TrueDepth camera, speaker, and microphone are all housed in a notch on the front display of the iPhone 13. This year's notch is narrower, allowing for a larger total display surface. The phone's top and sides feature antenna bands, as well as the power and volume/silence keys on the right and left, respectively. A 5G mmWave antenna is located beneath the power button, but it will only be available on iPhone models sold in the United States.

At the bottom of the iPhone 13 models are speaker holes and microphones, as well as a Lightning port for charging. The SIM card slot is on the device's left side.

The iPhone 13 models have a square camera bump on the back, as well as a new diagonal lens layout that differs from the iPhone 12's vertical lens array. The diagonal layout, according to Apple, enables new camera technology such as sensor-shift optical image stabilization.

Sizes

The iPhone 13 is available in two sizes: 5.4 and 6.1 inches, with the 5.4-inch iPhone 13 Pro being Apple's smallest iPhone. According to reports, this will be the final year for Apple to provide the smaller size, as its predecessor, the iPhone 12 mini, did not sell well.

The iPhone 13 and 13 mini are bigger and heavier than the iPhone 12 range.

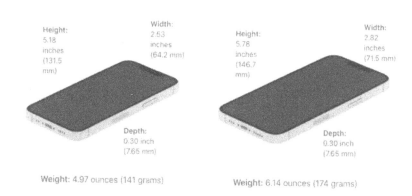

The iPhone 13 measures 5.18 inches tall (131.5mm), 2.53 inches wide (64.2mm), and 0.30 inch thick (7.65mm), while the iPhone 13 Plus measures 5.78 inches tall (146.7mm), 2.82 inches wide (71.5mm), and 0.30 inch thick (7.65mm).

At 4.97 ounces (141 grams), the small is the lightest phone in the iPhone 13 lineup, followed by the iPhone 13 at 6.14 ounces (174 grams).

Colors For several years, Apple has offered its regular iPhone lineup in a variety of vivid colors. Starlight (a blend of silver and gold), Midnight (black), Pink, Blue, (PRODUCT) RED, and Green, a new hue released in March 2022, are among the new colors available for the iPhone 13 and 13 mini.

Resistant to Water

The iPhone 13 and 13 mini are water-resistant to IP68 standards. Smartphones, like the iPhone 12 models, can endure a depth of up to six meters (19.7 feet) for up to 30 minutes.

The 6 in IP68 stands for dust resistance (meaning the iPhone 13 can withstand dirt, dust, and other particulates), and the 8 stands for water resistance. The maximum dust resistance grade available is IP6x. The iPhone 13 can withstand splashes, rain, and accidental water contact thanks to its IP68 water resistance rating, although purposeful water exposure should be avoided if at all feasible.

According to Apple, water and dust resistance are not permanent and can diminish over time as a result of natural wear. Because Apple's warranty does not cover liquid damage, it's best to avoid exposing your device to liquids.

Display

The same OLED Super Retina XDR display is found on all iPhone 13 variants, and it is flexible and stretches right into the device's chassis.

HDR photographs, videos, TV shows, and movies have a 2,000,000:1 contrast ratio for blacker blacks and brighter whites, as well as a peak brightness of up to 1200 nits.

The ordinary iPhone 13 models have a maximum brightness of 800 nits, which is 200 nits less than the Pro variants.

The 5.4-inch iPhone 13 small has a resolution of 2340 x 1080 pixels per inch and a pixel density of 476 pixels per inch, while the 6.1-inch iPhone 13 has a resolution of 2532 x 1170 pixels per inch and a pixel density of 460 pixels per inch.

Wide color support creates vibrant, true-to-life colors, and True Tone adjusts the display's white balance to match the ambient illumination for a more comfortable viewing experience. There's also a fingerprint-resistant oleophobic coating and Haptic Touch compatibility, which gives you haptic feedback when you interact with the screen.

Notch that is smaller

The notch that houses the TrueDepth camera system has been slimmed down by Apple, and it's now 20% smaller than previous iPhone models' notch. Comparisons of the iPhone 12 and iPhone 13 models show that the new notch is slightly taller than the previous one, despite being less wide.

Ceramic Shield

For the iPhone 13 models, Apple is sticking with the "Ceramic Shield" substance, which provides superior drop protection. Nano-ceramic crystals are infused into the glass to create the Ceramic Shield display cover. The display was created in collaboration with Corning, and the ceramic crystals were manipulated to optimize for clarity while maintaining toughness.

According to Apple, the Ceramic Shield is harder than any smartphone glass, with a dual-ion exchange technique that ensures scratch resistance and ordinary wear and tear.

Drop tests revealed no differences in durability between the iPhone 13 and iPhone 12 models, which is unsurprising given that they both have the same Ceramic Shield display and glass shell.

A15 Bionic Chip

All iPhone 13 models employ Apple's new A15 chip, which outperforms the A14 chip used in the iPhone 12 in terms of performance and economy. The A15 chip in the iPhone 13 models has two performance cores and four efficiency cores, and it is only topped by the version in the iPhone 13 Pro models.

The A15 CPU in the iPhone 13 and 13 mini has a 4-core GPU, one less than the A15 chip in the iPhone 13 Pro and Pro Max. As a result, the iPhone 13 Pro and Pro Max have the best GPU performance, albeit the regular iPhone 13 models aren't far behind.

In comparison to the iPhone 12 Pro models, the iPhone 13 Pro models have a 50% faster graphics performance, while the iPhone 13 models have a 15% faster graphics performance.

In terms of CPU performance, the iPhone 13 models are around 10% faster in single-core performance and approximately 18% faster in multi-core performance than the iPhone 12 models.

According to AnandTech's testing, the A15 is 62 percent faster than comparable devices and even faster than Apple's predictions.

Engine Neural

The 16-core Neural Engine, which powers features like Cinematic Mode and Smart HDR 4, can do up to 15.8 trillion operations per second.

RAM

The iPhone 13 variants come with 4GB of RAM, which

is two gigabytes less than the iPhone 13 Pro versions. The iPhone 13 has the same amount of RAM as the iPhone 12, whereas the iPhone 12 and 12 Pro models featured 4GB and 6GB of RAM, respectively.

Storage Areas

The iPhone 13 and the iPhone 13 mini both come with 128GB of storage as standard, while the iPhone 13 and iPhone 13 mini may be upgraded with up to 512GB of storage. That's half the storage capacity of the iPhone 13 Pro versions, which have up to 1 TB of storage.

TrueDepth Camera and Face ID

Face ID, a facial recognition technique that was initially unveiled in 2017, is used for biometric authentication on the iPhone 13 models. Face ID components are housed in the display notch's TrueDepth camera system, which is smaller this year.

Face ID is used to unlock the iPhone, grant access to third-party passcode-protected apps, confirm app purchases, and authenticate Apple Pay payments across all iOS operations.

Face ID is powered by a combination of sensors and cameras. A Dot Projector emits over 30,000 invisible infrared dots onto the skin's surface to create a 3D facial scan that maps each face's curves and planes, which is read by an infrared camera.

The A15 chip receives the facial depth map and converts it into a mathematical model that the iPhone employs to verify identity. Face ID works in low light and the dark, as well as with hats, beards, glasses, sunglasses, scarves, and other face-obscuring accoutrements, including hats, beards, glasses, sunglasses, scarves, and other scarves.

Using Face ID While Wearing a Mask

Users can use the "Unlock with Apple Watch" feature when wearing a face mask for further convenience. When wearing a mask, iPhone users can utilize an unlocked and authenticated Apple Watch as an alternative authentication mechanism to unlock their smartphone using Unlock with Apple Watch. It can't be used to verify Apple Pay or App Store transactions, and it can't be used to unlock apps that need a Face ID scan.

Apple enabled the ability for Face ID to function with face masks in iOS 15.4, eliminating the need for an Apple Watch to authenticate. For authentication purposes, Apple claims that the function can "recognize the unique features around the eye." You'll have to rescan your face for Face ID if you choose to use this function during setup. From then on, Face ID will be able to unlock your iPhone even if you're wearing a mask.

Face ID is "most accurate" when set up for full-face recognition exclusively, according to Apple's Settings app. Face ID with a mask requires that you look at your device to unlock it, and it does not work if you are wearing sunglasses. Unlike the previous Apple Watch Face ID feature, Face ID with a mask can validate Apple Pay payments and be used in place of a login and password in apps that support Face ID.

- What You Should Know: How Face ID with a Mask Works

- How to Set Up Face ID With a Mask on iOS 15.4

The new feature is only available on iPhones that are 12 years old or newer. iOS 15.4 is still in beta testing and has not yet been widely published to the public.

Features of the Front-Facing Camera

In addition to facial recognition, the TrueDepth camera system's 12-megapixel f/2.2 camera also serves as a front-facing selfie/FaceTime camera, with many of the same functions as the rear-facing camera.

Many of the photographic capabilities available with the rear cameras are supported by the A15 chip in the iPhone 13 models, including Night mode for selfies, Smart HDR 4, Dolby Vision HDR recording, and Deep Fusion, as well as ProRes and the new Cinematic Mode for capturing videos with a movie-like depth of field changes. Portrait Mode, Portrait Lighting, and the new Photographic Styles function for selectively applying edits are all supported. 4K video recording, QuickTake video, Slo-mo video, Portrait Mode, Portrait Lighting, and the new Photographic Styles feature for selectively applying edits are all supported.

Rear Camera with Dual Lenses

A diagonal dual-lens camera system is included in the iPhone 13 and 13 mini. The Ultra-Wide lens has an f/2.4 aperture, while the Wide lens has an f/1.6 aperture. The new Ultra-Wide camera performs better in low light, while the revised Wide camera lets in 47% more light.

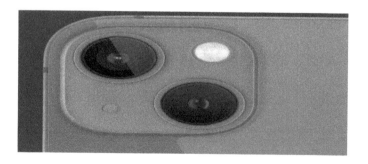

Because the iPhone 13 and 13 mini lack a telephoto lens, they can only zoom out 2x optically and up to 5x digitally.

Sensor-shift optical image stabilization, which was previously only available on the Pro models, is now available on all iPhone 13 models.

Features of the Camera

Smart HDR 4 recognizes up to four people in a scene and adjusts contrast, lighting, and skin tones to make everyone seem their best.

Photographic Styles: Photographic Styles are intelligent, programmable filters that may amplify or mute colors without changing skin tone. Unlike a filter, which is applied to the entire image, styles are applied selectively to an image. Vibrant (brightens colors), Rich Contrast (darkens shadows and deepens colors), Warm (accentuates golden undertones), and Cool are some of the photographic styles available (accentuates blue undertones). Each style's tone and warmth can be customized to achieve the precise look you desire.

Night Mode: takes a sequence of photographs over a few seconds and combines them to allow for photography in extremely dim lighting.

Deep Fusion: Brings out the texture and detail in images in mid-to low-light conditions.

Portrait Mode blurs the background while keeping the subject of the photo in focus.

Natural, Studio, Contour, Stage, Stage Mono, and HighKey Mono are some of the lighting effects available for Portrait Mode images.

When utilized, the built-in flash is designed to match the ambient lighting so that when utilized, the white balance of the photo is not thrown off.

Up to 63-megapixel panoramic pictures can be captured.

Burst Mode: Captures a succession of photos simultaneously, which is useful for high-action shots.

Making a video

On iPhone 13 models, up to 4K video recording at 24, 25, 30, and 60 frames per second is supported, as well as HDR video recording with Dolby Vision at 4K up to 60 frames per second. Video recording in 1080p and 720p resolutions are also accessible.

When taking video, there's a new Cinematic Mode that

employs rack focus to effortlessly transfer the focus from one topic to another. It keeps the topic in focus while blurring the backdrop, and it can adjust the focus automatically when a new subject enters the scene. The Photos app also allows you to change the blur and focus after you've captured the video. The cinematic mode supports Dolby Vision HDR and works with the Wide, Telephoto, and TrueDepth cameras.

QuickTake video, audio zoom, time-lapse, night mode, time-lapse, continuous focusing mode, 3x digital zoom, and the possibility to snap 8-megapixel photographs while recording 4K video are some of the other video capabilities.

The Life of the Batteries

With the A15 chip and higher battery capacity, Apple has increased battery life across the iPhone 13 lineup. The battery of the iPhone 13 mini lasts up to 1.5 hours longer than the iPhone 12 small, and the iPhone lasts up to 2.5 hours longer than the iPhone 12.

The iPhone 13 mini can play video for up to 17 hours (13 hours when streaming) and music for up to 55 hours. The iPhone 13 can play video for up to 19 hours (up to 15 hours streaming) and music for up to 75 hours.

The iPhone 13 has a 3,227 mAh battery, which is up from 2,815 mAh in the iPhone 12, while the iPhone 13 small has a 2,406 mAh battery, which is up from 2,227 mAh in the iPhone 12.

Using a Lightning to USB-C connector and a 20W power adapter, both iPhone 13 models feature rapid charging and can charge to 50% in 30 minutes.

5G Networking

In addition to LTE networks, the iPhone 13 models support 5G networks. The devices' 5G modems support both mmWave and Sub-6GHz 5G, the two forms of 5G, but mmWave speeds are still restricted to the United States.

The fastest 5G networks are mmWave networks, but because they are short-range and can be obscured by buildings, trees, and other obstacles, they are only used in major cities and urban areas, as well as venues such as concerts, airports, and other large gatherings.

Sub-6GHz 5G is becoming more common and accessible in cities, suburbs, and rural areas across the United States and other countries. When you use a 5G network, you'll almost always be using Sub-6GHz 5G. 5G at sub-6GHz is generally faster than LTE, but it's still in its early stages and isn't the super-fast 5G you might expect.

Faster download and upload rates are possible with 5G connectivity, which speeds up everything from loading webpages to downloading TV episodes and movies. It also improves FaceTime call quality and increases bandwidth for streaming services, so you can watch in higher resolution. FaceTime calls work in 1080p over 5G or WiFi. 5G frees up bandwidth and eliminates congestion in locations where LTE speeds are poor due to the sheer number of people, allowing for quicker usage speeds.

5G frequency bands

In the United States, iPhone 13 models support over 20 5G bands.

- mmWave 5G (Bands n1, n2, n3, n5, n7, n8, n12,

n20, n25, n28, n29, n30, n38, n40, n41, n48, n66, n71, n77, n78, and n79)

- 5G NR mmWave (Bands n1, n258, n260, and n261)

LTE frequency bands

In addition to 5G, the iPhone 13 models enable Gigabit LTE with 4x4 MIMO, allowing you to connect to LTE networks when 5G networks are unavailable. The bands listed below are supported:

- FDD-LTE (Frequency Division Duplex) is a (Bands 1, 2, 3, 4, 5, 7, 8, 11, 12, 13, 14, 17, 18, 19, 20, 21, 25, 26, 28, 29, 30, 32, 66, 71) wireless communication technology.

- TD-LTE stands for Terrestrial Digital Long-Term Evolution (Bands 34, 38, 39, 40, 41, 42, 46, 48).

Mode of Data Saving

When 5G speeds aren't required, Data Saver Mode switches the iPhone's connection to LTE in order to conserve battery life.

When the iPhone is updating in the background, for example, it uses LTE because ultra-high speeds aren't required, but when speed is critical, such as when downloading a show, the iPhone 13 models switch to 5G. There's also an option to use 5G instead of the automated Data Saver Mode whenever it's available.

Two SIM card slots are supported.

Dual SIM capability, which is enabled by the availability of a physical nano-SIM slot and an eSIM, allows two phone numbers to be used at the same time. Apple maintains a list of carriers that accept eSIM on its website, which is available in many countries across the world.

The iPhone 13 models are the first to allow Dual eSIM, which means that instead of only one eSIM and one nano-SIM, the iPhone 13 models may use two eSIMs at the same time. This year, Apple's iPhone 13 models that are tied to a carrier will not come with a physical SIM card, instead of relying on eSIM capabilities for activation.

Bluetooth, Wi-Fi, and U1 are all options.

The iPhone 13 models have an Apple-designed U1 chip that enables Ultra-Wideband technology for greater spatial awareness, allowing the iPhone 13 models to precisely locate other Apple devices equipped with the U1 chip. Because Ultra Wideband is designed for superior indoor positioning and location monitoring, Apple has compared it to "GPS on a living room size."

The iPhone 13 and 13 mini use the U1 chip to precisely track neighboring AirTags. It's also used for directional AirDrop and communication with the HomePod mini, which features a U1 chip as well.

The iPhone 13 versions feature Bluetooth 5.0 and Wi-Fi 6 in terms of connectivity (802.11ax).

Speakers are available as an option.

A stereo speaker is situated at the top of the iPhone 13 models, adjacent to the notch, while a second stereo speaker is located at the bottom, next to the Lightning connection.

Sensors

A barometer, a three-axis gyroscope, an accelerometer, a proximity sensor, and an ambient light sensor are all included in the iPhone 13 models.

NFC and GPS

GPS, GLONASS, Galileo, QZSS, and BeiDou location services are all supported on the iPhone 13 and 13 mini. The iPhone models have NFC with reader mode, as well as a background tag functionality that allows them to scan NFC tags without having to open an app first.

MagSafe

Built-in MagSafe technology is still available in the iPhone 13 series in the form of a magnetic ring that connects to the MagSafe charger and other magnetic accessories.

The MagSafe charger clips neatly into the back of the iPhone 13 models and charges at 15W, which is faster than Qi-based chargers' 7.5W wireless charging.

Other magnetic accessories, like cases, sleeves, snap-on wallets, and more, are compatible with the magnetic ring, and third-party firms can create MagSafe iPhone accessories as well.

Apple's MagSafe chargers have been known to leave a circular imprint on Apple's leather cases, while a similar effect has been noticed on silicone cases. According to Apple, credit cards, security badges, passports, and keyfobs should not be placed between the iPhone and the MagSafe charger.

The iPhone 13 models, like all iPhones, can cause interference with medical devices including pacemakers and defibrillators due to their MagSafe feature. Keep MagSafe iPhones and any MagSafe accessories a safe distance away from implanted medical devices, according to Apple.

Chapter 2

iPhone Won't Download Apps? 11 Methods to Fix It

It could be incredibly frustrating whenever your iPhone won't download apps. In the end, applications are part of the actual iPhone, so excellent. No matter whether you're aiming to download new applications or update applications you currently have, you want this to work. Fortunately, fixing this issue is not too difficult.

What Halts Apps From Installing on iPhone?

While mending an iPhone that won't download applications is not too difficult, what can cause the problem isn't quite so simple. Actually, there are almost as much potential factors behind this mistake as there are fixes for this. These range between App Store guidelines to simple insects, from issues with your Apple ID to your iPhone's configurations and more. Instead of providing a summary of the causes here, each solution below provides some history for the problem.

How To Fix An Iphone That Will Not Download Apps

If applications won't download to your iPhone, try these fixes, in this order.

- Try Wi-Fi. If you are aiming to download the application more than a mobile connection like 4G LTE, you may be hitting a restriction of the App Store. Apple limitations how big is app downloading over mobile to 150 MB. That is done to avoid users from using too much data about the same download. If the application you want to download is bigger than that, hook up to Wi-Fi. It is also smart to check to ensure you are not in Airplane Setting, which blocks all Wi-Fi and mobile network connections.

- Restart the App Store app. The insect in installing the app may need to do with the App Store application itself. If something will go wrong with this app, it will not have the ability to help set up the application you want. If so, restarting the App Store application may clear the insect. Then, just re-open the App Store application and make an effort to re-download the app.

- Pause and restart the application download. This suggestion only works on devices with a 3D

Touchscreen. It works whenever your application download has been interfered with for reasons unknown. If an application icon shows up on your home display, however the download seems sluggish or like it isn't occurring, hard press the icon for the application you're trying to set up. In the menu that pops right out of the icon, faucet Resume Download (whether it's already paused). You can do the same thing in the App Store app, on the display screen for the application you want to set up.

- Restart iPhone. Exactly like restarting the App Store application can solve the issue of apps not installing on your iPhone, sometimes you will need to restart all of your phone. This may be because the short-term glitch in your telephone could maintain the operating-system or another area of the phone's software. A restart will most likely resolve that type of issue.

- Check your Apple ID payment methods. To be able to download apps, you must have a payment method on document in your Apple ID. That is true even if you are aiming to download a free of charge app. So, unless you have a payment method on document, or if you have a card that's expired, you will possibly not have the ability to download apps. This may also business lead to a Confirmation Required pop-up message. Get yourself a valid payment method on document and you may be able to begin downloading applications again.

- Sign from the App Store and indication back. An iPhone that can't download applications may be considered an indication that something is up with your Apple ID. If the bond created by your Apple ID in the middle of your iPhone and the App Store gets disrupted, sometimes simply putting your signature on out and putting your signature on back will correct it. To achieve that, touch Configurations > iTunes & App Store > Apple ID

> Indication Out. Then, indication back by tapping *Register* and getting into your Apple ID account.

- Upgrade iOS. Whenever Apple produces an upgrade to the iOS - the operating-system that works on the iPhone, iPad, and iPod itouch - the new software fixes pests. Maybe your iPhone can't download applications due to an insect in the operating-system. A straightforward, fast, and free Operating-system revise may solve your trouble.

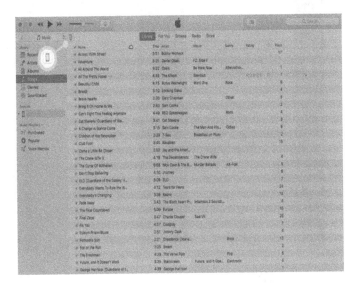

- Set correct day and time. Contrary to popular belief, but the time and time configurations on your mobile phone being incorrect can stop you from downloading apps. The simplest way to resolve this is to make your iPhone automatically arranged its day and time so that it is always correct. To achieve that, tap Configurations > General > Day & Time > move the Arranged Automatically slider on/green.

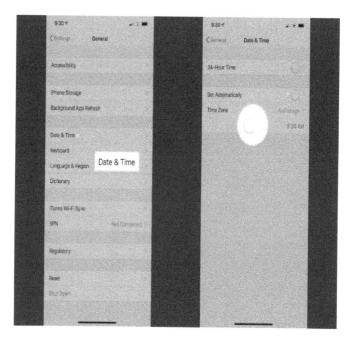

- Reset iPhone device configurations. Bugs like applications not installing on your iPhone can often be the effect of a small problem in your low-level configurations. You can't always see these configurations or fix them separately, however the iOS provides you ways to reset all configurations. Accomplishing this won't erase your computer data, but can solve these kinds of issues.

- Check the Apple ID you're using. If you are creating a problem upgrading an application already on your device, the problem may be the Apple ID you're using. When you download an app, it's linked with the Apple ID you're logged into at that time. In the event that you change the Apple ID you're using, applications linked with the old ID will not be able to upgrade. Try putting your signature on into other Apple IDs you've used, following an instruction in step 7 above.

- Get help from Apple. If you have tried many of these steps as well as your iPhone still won't download apps, you will need help from professionals at Apple. You may get online or telephone support via Apple's website or you may make a scheduled appointment at the Genius Pub at your neighborhood Apple Store for in-person help.

Chapter 3

How to Shut Down Apps on an iPhone

13

If your phone or apps are performing strangely, you may be able to address the problem by closing the problematic app. In this post, you'll learn how to view what apps are running on the iPhone 13 and how to close them.

Without a Home Button, How Do You Close Apps on an iPhone?

If you upgraded from an iPhone with a home button, you might be wondering how to check what apps are running or close apps on your iPhone 13 without a home button. Fortunately, Apple has included a set of gestures in iOS to replace the Home button. (You still have options if your home button is broken.)

To see what apps are running on iPhone models with a home button (the iPhone 8 and prior), double-click the home button. Simply slide up from the bottom of the screen on the iPhone 13 (and all iPhones without a Home button). All currently running apps will surface if you swipe roughly 10% of the way up the screen. To see them, simply swipe from side to side.

Many individuals believe that closing apps save memory and battery life. That is not the case. Only the app you're currently using consumes a substantial amount of memory (unless it's a background-only app like the Music app). So, even if you have 100 apps open at the same time, only the one you're currently using consumes a lot of RAM. It makes no difference if the other apps are closed. When it comes to battery life, closing apps too frequently can deplete it.

On my iPhone 13, how can I close all apps?

Any app running on your iPhone can be closed or terminated. As previously stated, you should only do this if an app is acting strangely, but if that's the case, here's how to close apps on the iPhone 13:

1. On any screen or app, swipe up from the bottom of the screen. It's only necessary to swipe up 10% of the way up the screen.

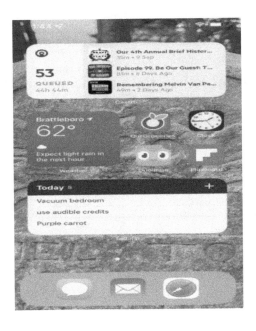

2. Your current app will be reduced in size and reverted to its previous state. You'll also be able to view which

other apps are now active.

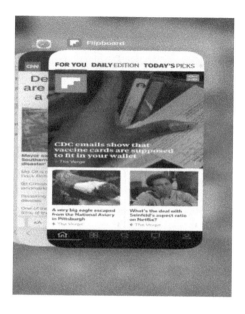

3. Swipe from left to right to locate the app you want to close.

4. Swipe the app you want to close from the top of the screen, then release it (as if it were a bug on the screen). The app has now been closed, but you can reopen it if you like.

Tips: You won't be able to close all of the apps on your iPhone with a single action. Even if you reset your phone, all of your apps will begin to run again as soon as it boots up. Closing up to three apps at once is the best option. Follow the first three steps from the previous section to do so. Step three involves tapping up to three apps with up to three fingers and then swiping them off the top of the screen.

What is the best way to see which apps are open on my iPhone 13?

Follow the first three steps from the previous section to see the apps running on your iPhone 13. You can see every open app, whether it's the active app or one that's in the background, by swiping side to side. In this layout, the app's name and icon are displayed above the app's top-left corner.

How to Record a Screen on an iPhone 13

Recording your screen activity is a terrific way to record important moments from games, illustrate operations on your iPhone, or troubleshoot applications and websites.

Is it possible to record video with the iPhone 13?

Screen recording is available on all iPhones running iOS 14 or later. You don't need to install any third-party programs to record your screen on iOS because it's a built-in capability. Screen recording isn't a standalone app, but it is an option in the Control Center, as we'll see.

How Do I Capture a Screen Shot on My iPhone 13?

Follow these instructions to record your iPhone 13's screen:

1. First, go to the Control Center and add the Screen Recording button. To do so, navigate to Settings > Control Center > Screen Recording and hit the Plus next to it.

2. Next, swipe to access the Control Center from the app or action you wish to record.

3. Tap the screen recording symbol (it's a solid dot with a circle around it) to begin recording right away. (Go straight to step 7.)

Tap and hold the screen recording icon to enable the microphone and choose where to save the recording.

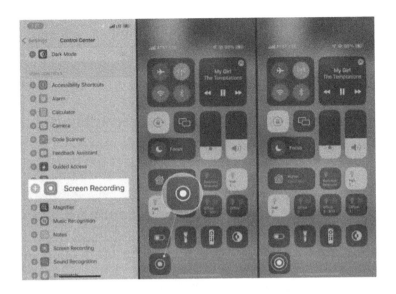

4. If you tap and hold the screen recording icon, a new screen displays, allowing you to control the recording's parameters.

To begin with, if more than one app on your iPhone allows you to save a screen recording, tap the one you wish to use to save the recording.

The iPhone's microphone is turned off by default during screen recordings, but you can turn it on to speak while the recording is being made. Toggle the microphone on or off by tapping the microphone icon.

5. Press the "Start Recording" button. A timer starts at 3 and counts down from there. The recording begins when the timer expires.

6. To end the screen recording, return to the Control Center and hit the screen recording icon once more. (If you have the screen recording controls set up as shown in step 5, hit Stop Recording.)

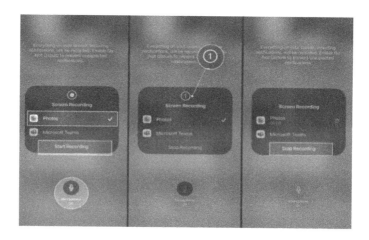

7. By default, screen recording videos are saved in the pre-installed Photos app's Videos album. Look for your

screen recording video there if you used a different program in step 5.

Why can't I record my iPhone 13's screen?

If you're having issues capturing your screen on your iPhone 13, attempt the following troubleshooting steps:

Note that you can screen record most, but not all, of the actions you undertake on your iPhone. Screen recording will be disabled for some activities, features, and apps due to security and copyright concerns. A streaming video app, for example, will normally not allow you to screen record because you may otherwise record a copy of the movie or TV show you're viewing. You can't capture sensitive data on the screen, such as entering your credit card number into Apple Pay.

There is no sound: If your videos don't have sound, make sure you turn on the microphone in step 5 above.

Can't record video during a game: If you're unable to capture a gameplay video, it's possible that a Screen Time setting is prohibiting you from doing so. If that's the case, go to Settings > Screen Time > Content & Privacy Restrictions > Content Restrictions > Screen Recording > Allow in the Game Center area.

Mirroring your screen: You can't screen record and use screen mirroring at the same time on the iPhone. If you try it, you won't be able to save a video.

Restart your iPhone: This easy step fixes a lot of temporary issues, so if screen recording isn't working and you're not sure why, restart your iPhone.

Update your operating system: An update to iOS may resolve issues with the screen recording feature in some circumstances, so update your operating system if a new version is available.

How to Use an iPhone 13 Smart Data Mode

If you don't want to utilize 5G all the time, turning on Smart Data can help you save battery life and reduce the amount of 5G data you use. To activate Smart Data mode, follow the instructions listed below.

- Open the Settings app on your iPhone.

- To get to the Cellular settings panel, tap Cellular.

- Select "Cellular Data Options" from the drop-down menu.

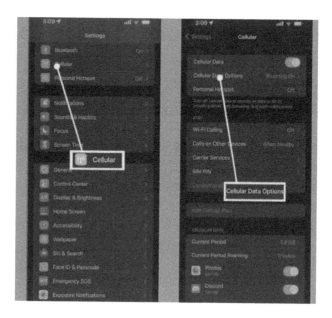

- Select "Voice & Data" from the drop-down menu.

- Select 5G Auto to enable Smart Data mode.

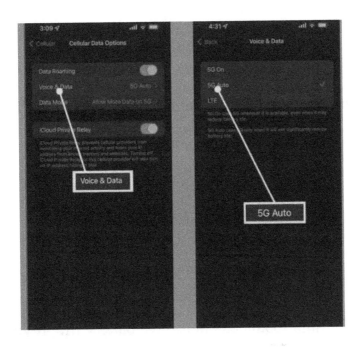

What Is the iPhone 13's Smart Data Mode?

On the iPhone 12, "Smart Data Mode" was introduced to address concerns that 5G data connections may reduce battery life. Smart Data mode was built by Apple to assist your phone in determining when to use 5G data and when LTE data is sufficient for the tasks at hand.

When Smart Data mode is turned on, your iPhone 13 will turn 5G on and off as needed. If your phone is in sleep mode and you aren't downloading anything, for example, it will turn off 5G to save battery life. If you open your phone and start downloading a movie, app, or TV show, it may switch to 5G to help speed up the process. When the display is off and you're downloading something in the background, your iPhone may use 5G.

How Do I Turn Off Smart Data Mode?

While Smart Data can help save battery life, if you live in a location where 5G isn't yet widely available—or if you simply want to utilize 5G all of the time—you can always use the other modes on your iPhone.

- Launch the Settings app on your iPhone 13.

- Select "Cellular Settings" from the drop-down menu.

- Select "Cellular Data Options" from the drop-down menu.

- Select "Voice & Data" from the drop-down menu.

- Select the 5G option if you want 5G to be active all of the time. Select LTE if you want to turn off 5G completely.

Chapter 4

How to Repair a good iPhone Glitch

Strategies for resolving normal iPhone problems. The iPhone will be the hottest smartphone, nonetheless, it is in no way perfect. A lot of customers report annoying display glitches along with other issues with no obvious cause. In case your iPhone is glitching, follow these pointers to recognize and repair the problem.

Glitches can be found in all sizes and shapes, and for you to repair this depends on the sort of glitch you're experiencing. Many problems have their very own set of possible solutions. Adhere to these troubleshooting suggestions, in order, to get your iPhone operating again.

Quit or close up issue apps. iOS occasionally crashes or leads to a variety of issues, but force-closing and relaunching apps frequently solve those difficulties.

Restart the iPhone. Restarting your iPhone can resolve a bunch of problems, which includes a frozen display screen. The guidelines for restarting an iPhone can be determined by your particular design.

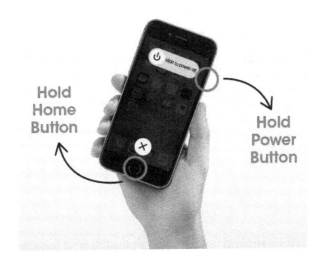

Update iOS. Frequently upgrading an iPhone may be the

most effective device to avoid glitches. Often, Apple company consists of fixes for recognized glitches that may be used by installing the brand new edition of iOS.

Register and from the Apple ID. A typical error is once the App Shop continuously refreshes but in no way loads. The ultimate way to stop this is to restart the phone. If it doesn't work, register and from the Apple Identification. *Select Configurations > iTunes & App Shop > Apple Identification,* then select Indication Out. Following that, use the same process to indicate back in.

Disable background refresh for apps you do not use or don't need to have. Even though you don't open up apps, numerous apps refresh in the backdrop, which may place pressure on the mobile phone and its electric battery, especially if you utilize information or processing-intensive apps. Head to *Configurations > Common > History App Refresh.* It is possible to disable history refresh for several apps or go for ones.

Disable automated updates. Apps that don't operate in the backdrop download updates instantly, and if there are lots of updates, it could slow down the phone. To shut this down, choose *Configurations > iTunes & App Shop.* Under Auto Downloads, toggle App Up-dates to off. You can even turn off automated updates for Songs, Apps, and Publications & Audiobooks.

Crystal clear the Safari cache. Every internet browser collects data as time passes to help it better to navigate the web. While hassle-free, the cache can sluggish a tool when it gets too big. To delete the cache, head to Configurations > Safari > Crystal clear History and Web site Data, then concur that you want to delete the info.

Look for iOS up-date and restore mistakes. Some glitches prevent you from upgrading iOS, which leads to error rules. While short and fairly cryptic, these rules show you the issue that prevents you from upgrading or restoring these devices. Consult Apple's set of upgrade and restore mistakes to get your error, after that follow the training to repair it.

Apple Pay might stop downloads until it is updated. If Apple Pay doesn't revise, take your phone into an Apple company store.

If you get an alert stating, ***"Cellular Update Failed,"*** this can be an issue using the phone's cellular modem. Go to an Apple company Shop or Genius Pub to repair it.

Try various Wi-Fi networks. If you are at work, college, or any other area where you register for the Wi-Fi every time you enter, this might interfere with Apple company up-dates. Use a general public Wi-Fi link or disable Wi-Fi if the app improves using a mobile connection. Head to Configurations > Wi-Fi, after that faucet the Wi-Fi toggle to disable Wi-Fi. Afterward, either discover and hook up to a new system or wait just a few minutes to reconnect to your present network.

Reset the system settings. When you have issues with Wi-Fi or mobile information, reset the system settings. You can even instruct these devices to forget a particular network, which causes the iPhone to disconnect from your network.

Reset the router. Restart your products in a string to diagnose the issue. At first, restart the iPhone. When the system problem persists, restart the Wi-Fi router, then your modem. If none of these solves the problem, there is most likely an outage together with your internet service supplier, and there is nothing you can do but wait.

Clear iCloud storage space or buy even more. In case your iPhone doesn't back up on iCloud, first, check out your storage configurations. Go to Configurations, select your title, then go for iCloud > Manage Storage space. In case your iCloud will be complete, download an iCloud power app to your personal computer and utilize it to download and backup files you no longer need immediate access to, such as old photos. Producing some space can solve several problems, or you can purchase more areas from Apple.

Clear the iPhone. Some gadgets, particularly old types, create hardware troubles as dirt and residue build-up. It is possible to clear, sanitize, and disinfect the phone but take care not to trigger damage along the way.

Troubleshoot the camera. In case your iPhone's digital camera is around the fritz, open up the App of the Digital camera and touch the flip symbol in the lower-right part to find out if both front side and back digital cameras are unavailable. Only if the rear digital camera is affected, take away the iPhone case and find out if it solves the problem. Some iPhones are not made with the rear digital camera in mind. Only when the front digital camera is affected, switch the phone off and cautiously clean the leading of the telephone with a dried out fabric. If both aren't working, restart these devices. If that's inadequate, there is most likely a hardware issue, and you'll have to get the iPhone for an Apple Store.

Protect your iPhone data. Hackers may try to hack, freeze, or sometimes glitch your iPhone, and the ultimate way to keep them out would be to protect your computer data and exercise safe conduct online. Don't open email messages or attachments on your phone if you are uncertain who sent the communications. The same will additionally apply to texts. Don't open texts from numbers you do not know.

Confirm that the thing is not hardware-related. The collection between a software program problem along a hardware concern can be slim. The simplest way to confirm it is not a software problem, or at the very least, not one it is possible to resolve, would be to inspect these devices for physical harm. Look for splits or distortions in the casing. If you discover any sign of physical harm impairing the telephone, go on to Apple company for repairs.

Get the iPhone from an Apple company Store. If none of the aforementioned tips resolved the issue, give the iPhone to some repair specialist or Apple company Genius Bar.

Try various Wi-Fi networks. If you are at work, college, or any other place where you register for the Wi-Fi each time you enter, this might interfere with Apple company up-dates. Use an open public Wi-Fi link or disable Wi-Fi if the app improves when using a mobile connection. Head to Configurations > Wi-Fi, after that faucet the Wi-Fi toggle to disable Wi-Fi. Afterward, either discover and hook up to a new system or wait just a few minutes to reconnect to your present network.

Make your iPhone do the job. The iPhone packages a huge amount of great features, nevertheless, you can make it even more effective by unlocking the iPhone hacks and methods hiding in your smartphone. You can find a huge selection of these key features, but listed below are our picks for that 15 greatest iPhone hacks.

01 Cost Your Electric battery Faster

Want to cost your iPhone's electric battery as fast as possible? Place it in Aircraft Mode first. Aircraft Mode tends off many top features of the phone, which includes mobile and Wi-Fi social networking, so there's much less for your battery to accomplish and it costs faster. Remember to turn Aircraft Mode off if you are done charging.

To use Aircraft Mode: Open Handle Middle (swipe down from the very best directly on iPhone X or more or upward from underneath on other choices) and faucet the aircraft icon.

Notice: This hack functions on all iPhone versions.

02 Shutting Apps Doesn't Save Electric battery Life

You might have heard that quitting apps helps your iPhone battery last longer. Regardless of how many individuals state it, it's not true. Quitting apps can make your electric battery require a recharge faster. So, don't stop apps you are not using-just keep them in the backdrop.

Take note: This hack functions on all iPhone versions.

03 Discover the Strongest Nearby Cellular Signal

Talk about a concealed feature! Neglect waving your mobile phone in the airflow and traveling to get the most powerful cellular signal. Simply use this technique and you'll get yourself a clear indicator of signal power:

- Open the telephone app.

- Dial *3001#12345#*.

- Tap the decision button.

- In iOS 6 through 10, this loads the Field Test display and you may skip to step 7. On iOS 11 or more, it loads the Primary Menu.

- Tap LTE.

- Tap Serving Cellular Meas to check out the ranges rsrp0 (your present cellular tower) and rsrp1 (the closest back-up tower).

- Tap the transmission strength indication in the very best left corner.

The lower the quantity, the higher the signal. Therefore -90 is a superb sign, -110 will be OK, and -125 is not good indication at all. Stroll around to observe how the transmission strength modifications and make use of your cell phone where you've got a low number.

Be aware: This hack functions on iPhones operating iOS 6 through iOS 10. On mobile phones working on iOS 11, your phone will need an Intel modem in it.

04 Create a Lighting Blink like a Notification

Need to get notifications of fresh texts, incoming phone calls, or some other useful info without looking at your iPhone display screen or hearing sounds? With this particular hack, the digital camera flash on the trunk of the phone blinks when you have a fresh notification. Just adhere to these actions:

- Tap Settings.

- Tap Common (skip this task on iOS 13 or more).

- Tap Accessibility.

- Tap Sound/Visual (neglect this step about iOS 13 or more).

- Tap LED Adobe to flash for Notifications (skip this task in iOS 13 or more).

- Proceed the slider to on. Also shift the Display on Silent slider to on.

Notice: This hack functions on all iPhone versions with a digital camera flash.

05 Take Photos With the Volume Button

Did you know that tapping the on-screen camera button isn't the only path to take pictures? There's an easier way to get photos rapidly, without considering or tapping the display. Once the Digital camera app is open, click on the volume up switch, and your mobile phone snaps a photo. This even works with headphones that have inline remotes.

Take note: This hack functions on all iPhone versions. Some models may take pictures with the button down, too.

06 Allow Siri To Help You To Take Photos

Everyone knows they can ask Siri queries but do you realize Siri could help you get photos faster? Although it can't capture the photo, Siri can open the Camera app towards the setting that you require, so you simply need to tap the camera button (or click on the volume button). Some tips about what to accomplish:

Activate Siri (hold straight down the house or Part button, based on your magic size) and have Siri to have a photo or video. Your alternatives are:

- "Hey Siri, have a picture" (you can even say "image")

- "Hey Siri, have a square picture"

- "Hey Siri, have a panoramic photograph"

- "Hey Siri, have a video"

- "Hey Siri, have a slow-motion movie"

- "Hey Siri, have a tap-lapse movie"

- "Hey Siri, have a selfie."

Once you have the image you need, touch the camera or volume button.

Be aware: This hack functions on all iPhone versions. The selfie function needs iOS 10 or more.

07 *Type Your Orders to Siri Rather than Speaking Them*

Siri is fantastic, nevertheless, you can't talk with Siri and obtain answers aloud in every scenario (and, for a lot of people with disabilities, speaking may not be a choice). In those cases, you should use Siri if you'll have Typed to Siri fired up. This trick enables you to access Siri and present it commands by typing. Some tips about what to accomplish:

- Tap Settings.

- Tap Common.

- Tap Accessibility.

- Tap Siri.

- Move the sort to Siri slider to on/environment friendly.

Right now, activate Siri, along with a keyboard seems to let you know your command. You can even speak utilizing the microphone icon.

Notice: This hack works on all iPhone models running iOS 11 or more.

08 Work with a Hidden Dark Mode

HINT: Using the launch of iOS 13, the official Black Mode continues to be put into the iPhone. Learn to utilize it by reading through How to Enable Black Setting on iPhone and iPad.

Dark modes certainly are a popular function for those who often make use of their devices at night. With the dark setting enabled, your iPhone user interface switches to darkish colors which are easier for the eye in low-light circumstances (they're also ideal for people with color blindness). As the iPhone doesn't provide a correct dark setting, this trick will get you petty near:

- Tap Settings.

- Tap General.

- Tap Accessibility.

- Tap Display Lodging.

- Tap Invert Colours.

- Pick either Wise Invert (which switches some on-screen colors to Dark Setting) or Vintage Invert (which switches all shades).

- It is possible to toggle the dark mode on / off easily.

Take note: This hack functions on all iPhone versions operating iOS 11 or more.

09 Put in a Virtual House Button for your Screen

When you have an iPhone X or newer version just iPhone 13, you may skip the old hardware Home key. Even though you possess another model, you may want your options and features to include a virtual House switch for your screen. This can be an excellent hack since it offers quick access to functions that otherwise need gestures or several taps. Make it possible for this virtual House key:

- Tap Settings.

- Tap Common.

- Tap Accessibility.

- Faucet Touch (just do this about iOS 13 or more).

- Tap AssistiveTouch.

- Shift the slider to on/natural.

Be aware: This hack functions on all iPhone versions.

10 Hidden Shortcuts For The Favorite Apps

When you have an iPhone having a 3D Touchscreen or an iPhone 11 or more, you can find shortcuts to standard features of a few of your preferred apps hidden in the app icons. To access them, difficult to push an app symbol. When the app helps this function, a menu pops right out of the image with a couple of shortcuts. Touch the one you would like and you'll leap into the app and into that actions.

Notice: This hack functions on the iPhone 6S collection, 7 collections, 8 collections, X, XS, XR, and 13 collections.

11 Help to make Far-Away Icons Better to Reach

As iPhone displays get bigger, getting icons at the corner of your hands gets harder. The iOS carries a function known as Reachability that pulls the very best symbols down the underneath of the display screen to make them simpler to the faucet. Here's how:

- On iPhones with a house button, gently dual touch (but don't click on) the house button.

- On the iPhone X or more, swipe down in the indicator line at the bottom of the display.

- The contents from the screen shift down.

- Tap that you would like and the display screen dates back to normal. If you have changed your mind, tap somewhere else on the display to cancel.

This hack works on the iPhone 6 series, 6S series, 7 series, 8 series, along with the iPhone X, XS series, XR, 11, 12, and 13 series.

12 substitute for your keyboard using a trackpad

We have a trick for you personally that makes puting the cursor in textual content easier. It functions by switching your keyboard right into a trackpad, just like the mouse on the laptop. Some tips about what to accomplish:

- Open up an app where you may edit the written text using the default iPhone keypad (quite a few third-party keyboards help this feature, as well).

- Tap and keep any key on the keyboard.

- The letters over the keys disappear. Pull your finger round the keypad like managing a mouse on the trackpad.

- View the cursor around the display screen and release once the cursor is where you need it to be.

Take note: This hack functions on iPhone versions having a 3D Touchscreen working iOS 9 or more, and on all the models operating iOS 12. On iOS 13, it is possible to just pull the cursor anyplace on the display; you don't need to hard push the keyboard.

13. Switch to Undo Typing

If you are typing an email, a text, or various other textual content and decide you intend to erase what you've simply written, you don't have to utilize the delete button on the keyboard. When you have this hack allowed, all you have to do will be switch your iPhone to delete whatsoever you have typed. Here's what to accomplish:

- Tap Settings.

- Tap Accessibility.

- Touch (in iOS 13 or more only).

- In the Interaction section, tap Shake to Undo.

- Proceed the slider to on/environment friendly.

- After that, whenever you've simply typed

something you intend to remove, shake your cell phone and faucet Undo in the pop-up window.

Be aware: *This hack functions on all iPhone versions.*

14. *Equalize Songs Quantity When One Touch*

Ever observe that the songs on your cell phone are recorded at various volumes? Old tunes are often quiet, newer tunes are often louder. This may mean that you must change the quantity regularly. Well, we have a trick that makes all your songs play at the same degree. It's called Audio Check and it's included in the iOS. It inspects the quantity on all your songs finds the average and applies that to your songs automatically. Here's how to enable it:

- Tap Settings.

- Tap Music.

- Scroll right down to Playback.

- Move the Noise Examine slider to on/natural.

- This hack works on all iPhone models.

15. *Measure Areas Making use of Augmented Reality*

You might understand that your iPhone includes a built-in Level you should use to straighten pictures or shelves, but did you also know, it comes with an app called Gauge that uses Augmented Reality to assist you to measure distances? Some tips about what you must do:

- Tap the Gauge app to open up it.

- Place your iPhone camera so that it's dealing with a flat surface area.

- Touch the + symbol to start calculating.

- Shift the iPhone for the screen to also moves.

- When you've measured the area, touch the + once again showing the measured range.

Notice: The Gauge app can perform better than this.

How to Cancel Subscriptions on iPhone

Manage your iTunes and App Store subscriptions from your phone. Apple company makes it super-easy to subscribe and make use of the apps credit card or debit cards together with your Apple company ID. Once you no longer like those providers, canceling the subscriptions is a little trickier. Nevertheless, it is possible to cancel membership on both iPhone and in iTunes or the Songs app on the computer.

Take note: The directions in this specific guide connect with iPhones, iPads, and iPod iTouch devices working on iOS 15, iOS 14, and iOS 13. Also, they apply to computer systems operating on iTunes 12, also to the Songs app in macOS Catalina (10.15), as indicated.

About Subscriptions

Subscriptions that you join with the App Store with an iPhone or even iTunes on the computer are associated with your Apple Identification, rendering it possible for you to access them from several devices. They are regular monthly or yearly subscriptions to solutions and apps offering things like registering for Netflix or Hulu utilizing their apps, unlocking reward top features of an otherwise-free app, or for Apple's subscription services, such as Apple Songs and News.

Apple charges your account monthly or yearly once it's time for you to renew your subscription using the credit score or debit credit card you might have on a document with Apple.

You've probably experienced a free test period having an app that renews immediately by the end of the demo period if you don't cancel it. Unless you cancel, Apple charges you. Whether you intend to prevent this sort of not-so-free cost or have become tired of something that you've already been paying for frequently, it is possible to cancel your membership.

Note: You need to cancel the registration at least twenty four hours before the renewal time.

How to Cancel a Membership on iPhone

Just as everyone else could subscribe to an iPhone, it is possible to cancel subscriptions presently there, too. To achieve that, though, you do not use the app you're using to cancel. Rather, follow these measures:

- Touch the Settings app for the iPhone Home display screen to open it up.

- Touch your Apple ID.

- Touch Subscriptions to open up the Subscription configurations screen.

- Tap the registration that you would like to cancel. This display lists all your present subscriptions in the Energetic area as well as your canceled or expired subscriptions in the Expired area.

- Tap Cancel Membership. This screen also contains other options of the subscription.

- In the pop-up window, tap Confirm to cancel the subscription.

- You can even access the Subscription settings by tapping the App Store app on the iPhone Home screen. Touch your image near the top of the App Store screen and faucet Subscriptions to open up the same Subscription configurations you access with the Settings app. After that follow Actions 4 through 6 above.

Note: Once you cancel the subscription, it is possible to still use it until the end of the existing subscription period (usually per month or even 12 months). This is noted at the bottom of the screen under the Cancel button.

How to Cancel Subscriptions on the Computer

You can even cancel your subscriptions using iTunes on the Mac using macOS Mojave (10.14) or previous or on the Personal computer with iTunes 12. Here's how:

- Open iTunes.

- Click Account in the menus bar and choose View My Accounts in the drop-down menus.

Note: Mac customers working macOS Catalina (10.15) don't possess iTunes. They achieve their accounts by clicking on the Songs app and choosing Account in the proper sidebar. Besides that, the process is equivalent to iTunes.

- Enter your Apple company ID account when prompted.

- Scroll right down to the Settings area and select Manage close to Subscriptions.

- Click Edit close to the membership you intend to cancel.

- This screen lists all active and expired subscriptions you might have.

- Click on Cancel Subscription and confirm the cancellation in the pop-up window.

Note: It is possible to cancel iTunes subscriptions on your Apple TV, as well. To achieve that, go to Configurations > Customers & Accounts. Choose your accounts and head to Subscriptions. Choose the service you intend to cancel and select Cancel Subscription.

How To Print From Your iPhone With Airprint

Connect your phone or other Apple devices wirelessly to some printer. From your document, tap Share > Print > Select Printer under Printer Options > tap the inkjet printer you need > Print.

112

It is possible to connect your iPhone along with other Apple company devices to some printer to print files stored on your phone, iPad, and/or even iPod touch.

You need to be using an Airprint-supported app, linked to an Airprint-supported printer, and on a single Wi-Fi network.

How to Make use of AirPrint

To print the document with an iOS device making use of AirPrint:

- Open, the record, photo, email, or other files that you would like to print.

- Tap Talk about, then tap Print out.

Note: When the Printing option isn't in the list, swipe to the bottom of the symbols to display even more options. If it's not with this checklist, the app might not support printing.

- In the Printer Options display, tap Select Printer.

- In the Printer display screen, tap an inkjet printer.

- Touch the + and - control keys to set the number of copies to printing.

Note: With regards to the printer, additional options may be obtainable, for instance, double-sided printing, color selection, and web page varies for multi-page files.

- When you have made your choices, faucet Print.

- The record will go directly to the printer.

Requirements for Making use of AirPrint

The iPhone does not have a USB port, and can't be connected to the printers with cables just like a desktop computer or laptop. Instead, it utilizes AirPrint. AirPrint is a wireless technology included in every iOS gadget that makes use of Wi-Fi and suitable printers to printing from your iPhone. To utilize AirPrint from an iOS gadget:

- Setup an AirPrint-compatible inkjet printer. Not

absolutely all printers works with AirPrint, examine Apple's listing before you get.

- Link the iOS device and inkjet printer to the same Wi-Fi system. An iPhone linked to a functioning system cannot print to some printer linked to a home system, for example.

- Install an app that facilitates AirPrint around the iOS device.

Pre-Loaded iOS Apps That Support AirPrint

The next Apple-supported apps pre-loaded in the iPhone, iPad, and iPod iTouch that support AirPrint:

- Mail

- Maps

- Notes

- Photos

- Safari

Apple ID Handicapped? Fix-It Quick!

Learn why you're disabled and how to go forward. Having an operating Apple ID is vital to making use of your iPhone or any Apple device, so a handicapped Apple ID is a problem. For the reason that situation, you will not have the ability to do things such as buy apps through the App Store or update your Apple Identification billing or membership information. A handicapped Apple ID may seem like a large problem, but you can fix it.

How to find out if your apple ID is still disabled

Whenever your Apple ID is disabled, the Apple device tells you. You will not have the ability to perform the actions that need an Apple Identification, and you'll observe on-screen information informing you of the issue. The exact information may be various, but the most typical ones are usually:

- This Apple ID is disabled for security reasons.

- You can't register because your account was handicapped for protection reasons.

- This Apple ID is secured for security reasons.

- If you notice these alerts, Apple handicapped your Apple ID.

Reasons Why a good Apple Identification Is Disabled

Apple company automatically disables Apple users IDs when somebody tries to sign-in too many occasions using the wrong password, security query, or other username and passwords. This can occur if you neglect your security password or accidentally use the wrong security password too many times. Much more likely, though, somebody is trying to get unauthorized access to your Apple ID.

A typical hacking technique is named a Brute Pressure Attack, which functions by logging directly into a merchant account with guesses for passwords. Instead of allowing that to occur and potentially place your account at an increased risk, Apple company disables the Apple company ID account that could be a hacker's focus on after several incorrect entries. After that, only an individual who is the owner of the accounts and knows the proper info can reactivate it.

Whenever your Apple ID is disabled, you can't sign in (despite having the right password) and soon you reenable the accounts.

How to Repair a Disabled Apple user ID

Reenabling your handicapped Apple ID needs likely to visit the Apple website and reset your password. As long as you're there, start two-factor authentication, if you haven't currently, for added safety from potential hackers.

- Go directly to the iForgot.appleuser.com website.

Note: If you entered the incorrect password frequently after your accounts were disabled, you likely have to wait each day and night before you unlock your Apple company ID.

- Enter your account with your Apple Identification username.

- Enter your contact number and click Carry on.

Apple company sends notifications to the gadgets associated with your Apple Identification to enable you to reset your security password. Unless you possess access to some other products, click Don't possess access to all of your gadgets? at the bottom of the screen.

Whichever option you select, follow the on-screen prompts to unlock your accounts or reset your security password. Reactivating your Apple user ID takes more time unless you have got access to all of your devices.

Two-Factor Authentication Gives a Step

Apple company encourages customers of its items to add safety to their balances through the use of two-factor authentication making use of their Apple user ID. With this particular approach, it is possible to access your Apple user's ID only when you might have your account and an arbitrarily generated code given by Apple company.

By using two-factor recognition, fixing your handicapped Apple ID is nearly like when you avoid it. The only real difference is that you'll require access to the devices you selected when you set up the two-factor authentication.

Apple company sends the arbitrary code compared to that gadget during the procedure for unlocking or resetting your Apple company ID.

Note: *If you changed your security password whilst reenabling your Apple user ID, get your Apple ID making use of your new security password on all of your devices, which includes iCloud, FaceTime, and elsewhere.*

Chapter 5

How to Use Cinematic Mode on the iPhone 13

This guide will show you how to use Cinematic Mode on your iPhone 13 and walk you through the different customization choices available when recording video in this mode.

What Is Apple's Cinematic Mode, and How Does It Work?

The iPhone 13 comes with Apple's Cinematic Mode, a new video function. When activated, it allows the device user to add rack focus to their videos automatically, effectively creating a depth of field in videos. By deciding on which target the recording should focus on, the recording appears more professional and cinematic.

While you can determine the point you wish to center on when recording the video, you can also edit the focus target after the recording has been done. You can also adjust where the emphasis moves, allowing you to swiftly switch between focus targets.

On my iPhone, how can I activate Cinematic Mode?

If you have an iPhone 13, Cinematic Mode can be accessed directly from the camera app on your phone. You won't be able to use Cinematic Mode if you have an iPhone 12 or earlier. If you have an iPhone 13 and are having issues with the Cinematic Mode, make sure you have the most recent iOS version installed. Then, to begin using Cinematic Mode, follow the steps below.

- Launch the Camera app on your iPhone 13.

- Swipe left on the mode selection bar until "Cinematic" appears.

- Cinematic Mode can now be used to record videos.

Making Use of Cinematic Mode

Before you begin filming movies with the new Cinematic Mode, familiarize yourself with the many controls available to you. Several options can be explored and understood from the recording screen. To access the depth of field settings, press the f symbol on the button. This can be changed in any way you like. When recording, it will have a direct impact on how blurry the background behind your focal item seems (you can also change this later on during editing).

If you have an iPhone 13 Pro or Pro Max, you can also use the 1x button to switch between the telephoto and wide lenses included in your device. You may also rapidly modify the exposure on the recording by tapping the plus and minus sign buttons.

Is there a cinematic mode on the iPhone 13?

Cinematic Mode is built right into the camera app on every device in the iPhone 13 family. The iPhone 13, iPhone 13 mini, iPhone 13 Pro, and iPhone 13 Pro Max are the models.

While Cinematic Mode is available on all iPhone 13 models, only the iPhone 13 Pro and iPhone 13 Pro Max will have the option to switch to the telephoto lens before beginning a recording. All other models, on the other hand, can still take advantage of the new recording mode's depth of field features.

Is the iPhone 13 a water-resistant device?

Cinematic mode and a 120Hz refresh rate are among the interesting features of the Apple iPhone 13 series. Another key feature shared by all iPhone 13 models is dust, splash, and water resistance—within certain limits. As a result, the iPhone 13 is water-resistant but not waterproof.

Is the iPhone 13 a water-resistant device?

The iPhone 13 isn't waterproof, so don't expect it to be. All iPhone 13 models, however, including the iPhone 13, iPhone 13 mini, iPhone 13 Pro, and iPhone 13 Pro Max, have an IP68 classification for ingress protection.

IP ratings fall under the International Electrotechnical Commission (IEC) 60529 standard, which measures how well electronics hold up to dust and moisture. For electronics, IP ratings are the industry standard. IP ratings can be found on headphones, smartwatches, and a variety of other personal electronics.

There are two elements to IP addresses:

- *Dust protection:* The first number on the scale ranges from no protection (zero) to completely sealed off (six).

- *Moisture resistance:* The second value ranges from no seal (zero) to complete protection from multiple angles of water pressure—including hot water (nine).

The IP68 designation on the iPhone 13 signifies that it is

dust-resistant and water-resistant, but not completely waterproof.

What does that imply in practice? Whether you put your phone in a pool by mistake or take it into the water on purpose, your iPhone 13 should be fine.

Apple claims that all four iPhone 13 models can be submerged and protected for up to 30 minutes in water up to 6 meters deep.

Is there a water-resistant iPhone?

Although no iPhone is completely waterproof, numerous versions after the iPhone 7 have water resistance. Several recent iPhone models have water resistance that is comparable to or better than that of the iPhone 13.

The following models have the same IP68 protection against splashing, dust, and immersion in up to 6 meters of water for up to 30 minutes:

- iPhone 12

- iPhone 12 mini

- iPhone 12 pro

- iPhone 12 Pro Max

Note: If your iPhone has been exposed to or dipped in water, Apple recommends gently tapping it against your hand with the lightning connector facing down to dry the device. You should also avoid charging or using your iPhone's Lightning port until it's completely dry.

Some iPhones have an IP68 rating as well, although they can't be submerged as deeply. These variants provide IP68 protection for 30 minutes in up to 4-meter depths:

- The Apple iPhone 11 Pro

- The iPhone 11 Pro Max from Apple

Other iPhones can only endure 2-meter depths for a

maximum of 30 minutes. This list includes the following items:

- The iPhone 11 from Apple

- iPhone XS

- iPhone XS Max

Several older iPhones cut back the water-resistance further with an IP67 rating. This grade provides dust protection as well as 30-minute submersion in 1-meter depths.

- Apple iPhone SE (2nd generation)

- iPhone XR,

- iPhone X,

- iPhone 8

- iPhone 8 plus

- iPhone 7

- iPhone 7 plus

Note: The iPhones listed above can resist spills from coffee, tea, and juice daily. If you need to clean your phone, Apple suggests avoiding soaps or detergents.

Is the iPhone 13 capable of taking underwater photos?

While iPhone 13 models can withstand submersion in 6-meter depths for 30 minutes, you should probably think twice before taking your phone snorkeling without protection.

Nothing should be left to chance. Invest in a waterproof case for your iPhone 13 to protect it from the elements.

In shallow water, a simple plastic case might suffice. Depending on the type of images you wish to take, heavier-duty aluminum cases with a waterproof seal or mounting systems and lens attachments maybe even better.

How to Use Apple Pay on an iPhone 13

Apple Pay is a contactless, fast, and secure way to pay for purchases in shops and online. This guide will show you how to utilize Apple Pay on your iPhone 13 and how it works.

Is it possible to use Apple Pay on an iPhone 13?

The iPhone 13 may use Apple Pay in stores that accept it and have appropriate payment terminals, just like all iPhone models since the iPhone 6 series. You'll need the following to utilize Apple Pay on the iPhone 13:

- An Apple Pay-enabled debit or credit card from a bank.

- Sign up for Apple Pay using your debit or credit card.

- Turn on Face ID on your iPhone 13.

- Your iPhone is signed in to iCloud.

On my iPhone 13, how do I use Apple Pay?

If you've completed all of the prerequisites in the preceding section and are ready to use Apple Pay on your iPhone 13, proceed as follows:

- When you're ready to pay in an Apple Pay-enabled store, wait until the clerk says it's time to pay. A light on the credit card terminal usually signifies that it is ready for payment.

- Press and hold the iPhone's side button twice.

- Bring your iPhone 13 up close to the payment terminal.

- Use Face ID to approve the purchase by glancing at your iPhone's screen.

Tips: If you're wearing a mask and can't use your Face ID to authenticate, wait until Apple Pay expires. Then tap Pay with Passcode and input your iPhone passcode to complete the purchase.

- The iPhone screen will display a "Done" tick, and the payment terminal will proceed to the next stage. In some situations, you may be required to enter your debit card PIN.

Apple Pay on iPhone 13: How to Set It Up

Do you want to set up Apple Pay on your iPhone 13?

Take the following steps:

- Open the Wallet app.

- Press the "Plus" button

- Select "Debit or Credit Card" from the drop-down menu.

- Select the Continue option.

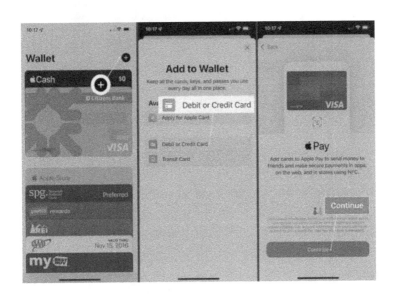

- Place your credit card in the screen's viewfinder, and the Wallet app will recognize and add it. Tap

Next after verifying the card number.

- Tap "Next" after verifying the expiration date and entering the three-digit security code.

- Agree to the conditions of the agreement.

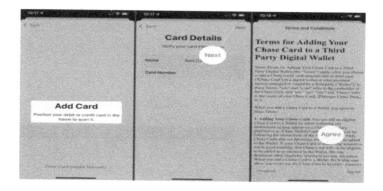

- Choose whether or not to make the new card your default (you'll only need this if you have multiple Apple Pay cards) and whether or not to add the card to Apple Pay on your Apple Watch.

- When you tap Done, the card will be available in your Wallet app for use with Apple Pay.

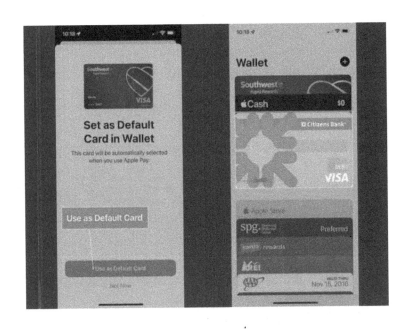

What Is Apple Pay and How Does It Work on the iPhone 13?

Apple Pay uses a combination of Near-Field Communications (NFC) and Apple software and services to transport data wirelessly.

Apple Pay is more secure than using a debit or credit card since it never sends the vendor your real card number. Instead, for each purchase, Apple Pay generates a one-time, disposable card number. Apple has access to your one-time card number as well as your actual card number. When money is sent from your account to a merchant, it first goes through Apple's servers, where the one-time and real card numbers are matched to complete the transaction while respecting your privacy, and then to the merchant.

NFC, a short-range wireless networking technology used for payments and device tracking, is used for the final stage in the process: transmitting data from your phone to the merchant's payment terminal.

How to Use Siri on the iPhone 13

This is a guide on how to use Siri on the iPhone 13, it operates similarly to how Siri works on other iPhones. The following procedures will work on all iPhones running iOS 15, the iOS version launched with the iPhone 13.

What is the best way to use Siri on my iPhone 13?

You'll need to make sure Siri is enabled on your iPhone 13 before you can utilize it. Open Settings > Siri & Search on your iPhone 13 to activate Siri.

If you want to use Siri with your voice, toggle on "Listen" for "Hey Siri," and if you want to use Siri with a button, toggle on "Press Side Button for Siri."

- If your iPhone is listening for voice commands, saying "Hey Siri" will launch Siri and prepare your iPhone for a question or command. Always talk loudly near your iPhone, but keep in mind that iPhones are notoriously good at picking up voices.

Note: Place your iPhone face down if you only want to utilize Siri's voice control occasionally. The iPhone will no longer listen for the Siri wake phrase if you do this.

- The iPhone 13's side button is used to activate Siri

with a button rather than by voice. If you press and hold the side button, Siri will open. After that, you can ask any question you want or issue a command.

Note: This technique is the same if you're using an earlier iPhone running iOS 15, but if your iPhone includes a home button, you'll need to press and hold the home button to access Siri.

- To access Siri with EarPods and an iPhone 13, press and hold the center or call buttons. If you're using AirPods with an iPhone 13, you can also access Siri by saying "Hey Siri" while wearing your AirPods.

Note: Depending on the AirPods you're using with the iPhone 13, you might be able to activate Siri with a button on the AirPods. However, whatever button you press depends on your AirPods model. To see if Siri works with AirPods, go to Apple's support website.

- After asking Siri a question or delivering a command, you may either hit the listen button or speak "Hey Siri" again to send out another order or ask another inquiry. You can restate or spell out a request by tapping the Listen button, and you can amend the language immediately by tapping your request onscreen.

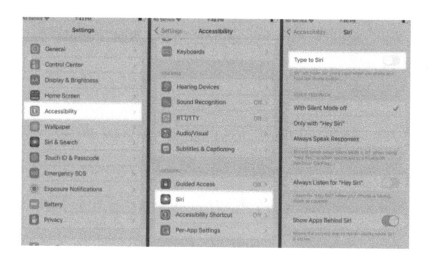

Note: If you'd rather type to Siri than speak to her, go to
Settings > Accessibility > Siri and enable "Type to Siri."
Once Siri is open, you'll see a text field where you may
type in your inquiries or orders.

How to Perform a Factory Reset on an
iPhone 13

You should factory reset your iPhone before sending it in
for service, selling, or giving it away to protect your data
and privacy.

How Do I Force a Factory Reset on My iPhone 13?

Simply follow these steps to factory reset an iPhone 13 running iOS 15 or higher:

- Create an iPhone backup. Because this is a phase in the factory reset procedure, it's best to be extra cautious. After all, this is your priceless information. Find out how to back up your iPhone.

- Go to Settings.

- Select "General."

- Tap "Transfer or Reset iPhone" at the bottom of the screen.

- Select "Erase All Content and Settings" from the menu.

- This page indicates what data will be deleted from your iPhone, including your Apple ID and the Activation Lock for this iPhone (important if you're selling it!). Continue by tapping the Continue button.

- If prompted, enter your iPhone's passcode or Apple ID.

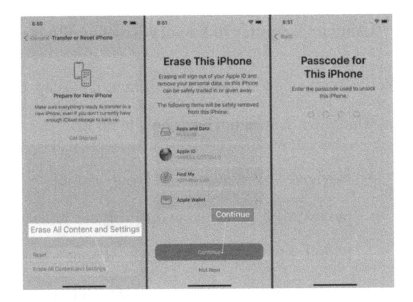

- Your iPhone's data will be backed up to iCloud. Again, you'll probably want to restore your backed-up data onto your new iPhone, so make a backup (or when you get the current one back from being repaired). Once the backup is complete, follow any onscreen prompts that remain.

- The data on your iPhone will be erased. You've completed the iPhone 13 factory reset when the iPhone restarts and displays the first setup screen.

Using a Computer to Factory Reset an iPhone 13

You can also factory reset your iPhone 13 using the PC on which you synced it. Here's how to do it:

- Navigate to Settings > [your name] > [your password] > [your password] > [your password] > ["Find My" >"Find My" My iPhone" Slide the Find My iPhone slider to off or white to turn off Find My iPhone on your phone.

- Use a USB cord to connect your iPhone 13 to your computer.

- On a Mac running macOS 10.15 (Catalina) or later, open a new Finder window and select your iPhone under Locations. Open iTunes on a PC or an older Mac.

- Select "Restore iPhone" from the main iPhone management panel.

146

- Decide whether you want to backup your iPhone. It comes highly recommended!

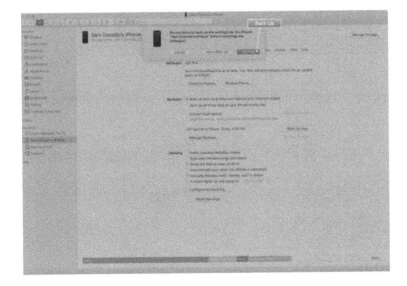

- Select "Restore" from the menu.

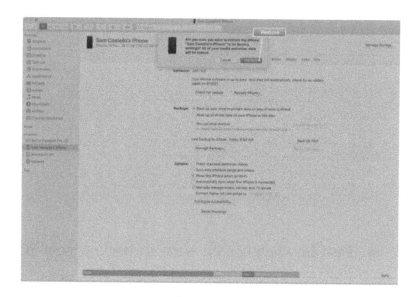

- When your iPhone 13 restarts and returns to the setup screen, it has been factory reset.

Is the iPhone 13 equipped with a factory reset button?

To initiate a factory reset, there is no physical button or combination of buttons to push. This is done on purpose since you don't want to be able to factory reset your iPhone by tapping the wrong buttons.

However, pressing buttons can be used to do some necessary iPhone maintenance, such as restarting or hard

148

resetting an iPhone and entering Recovery Mode.

Using Macro Photography on an iPhone 13

How to Use Macro Mode on the iPhone 13 Pro

When the iPhone 13 Pro and Pro Max recognize that you are close to an object, macro mode is automatically enabled until you disable it. So, if you notice a beautiful flower, for example, open the camera app and get closer to it. When you get close enough, the phone will go into macro mode. When you move away from the phone, it will revert to normal camera mode.

On the iPhone 13, where is the macro setting?

Because some people find the automatic move to macro mode disturbing, iOS has included a new setting to disable it.

- Launch the Settings application.

- Go to the bottom of the page and select "Camera."

- At the bottom of the page, toggle Auto Macro on and off.

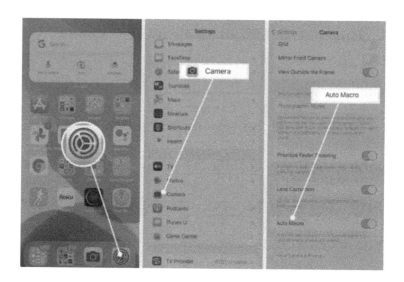

If you disable this feature, you can still use the ultra-wide lens for photos, but it will not swap automatically. Simply press the button in your camera's viewfinder to switch to the ultra-wide lens.

Chapter 6

How to Know If Someone Blocked You On iPhone

Not getting through? You may be clogged. There isn't any foolproof solution to learn if someone will be blocking your phone calls on the iPhone beyond looking at the telephone and looking at the set of obstructed numbers. However, there are a few definite signs that may hint that they've clogged you.

The ultimate way to know if somebody blocked you and what you need to ask them

In case your calls have gone unanswered as well as your texts and you didn't get yourself a reply, you need to just inquire further outrightly: Did you block me personally on your phone? There is an opportunity they do and didn't imply. If you are uncomfortable requesting them if they've obstructed you, attempt these ideas.

On How Many Occasions Did Your Contact Ring?

The largest indicator of the blocked call is a solitary ring that would go to voicemail. Nevertheless, this won't mean you're certainly being clogged. If your partner is utilizing their phone at that time, particularly if they're speaking with someone else, they can choose to take or decline the decision. This can clarify a contact that quickly would go to voicemail. Another feasible straight-to-voicemail situation is usually if another person's phone is switched off or the electric battery is drained.

The iPhone includes Do Not Disturb mode that could interfere with your call getting through. When the receiver has this fired up, the phone contact won't ring before going to voicemail. If it ring once and the next thing you hear is voicemail information, it's most likely to happen due to Usually Do Not Disturb.

Send a TEXT

The iPhone can send read receipts, this means it tells you if the individual browses the message. Is not everyone that offers this fired up, so it's furthermore not a certain way of knowing if you're obstructed, but it will be a good method of discovering if you're not blocked.

When you deliver a voice note to a pal which has you blocked, the standing will quickly consider Delivered working for you, but your buddy will never have the message. As a result of this, they can not read your information. Check back again after one hour or so; when the position has transformed from Sent to Read, they're not blocking you.

Contact With Caller Identification Disabled

Here is a sneaky technique. Disable Caller Identification. In the United States, dial *67 while followed by telephone numbers, such as *675551239870. Do that immediately after getting the telephone call head to voicemail following a solitary ring to find out if they find solution to the unknown contact.

Outside The United States, check out the Caller ID on Wikipedia web page for the rules to disable Caller ID. Not absolutely all countries permit Caller ID to be disabled, and also in nations that enable it, it can not be deactivated on phone calls to emergency figures such as 911.

You can even disable Caller ID. Open up Settings from your iPhone, scroll right down to Cell phone, and switch off Display My Caller ID.

Also, this doesn't mean your buddy blocked you. Lots of people refuse to respond to phone calls without Caller ID, and also if it rings once and would go to voicemail, they could have immediately dropped the call.

The sneakiest solution to tell if you are being blocked would be to contact the person

Whenever you see the person, call them. This is most effective if you are with several people and the individual has their cell phone out. If you contact and there is no indicator on the telephone or from your friend that the decision is being positioned, they probably have you blocked.

Remember, a cell phone in a wallet or handbag could be on vibrate setting, which explains why it is critical to contact the recipient whilst their phone has gone out.

How to Crystal clear Your iPhone Cache

Get the iPhone working faster, at this time. The iPhone instantly creates hidden documents during day-to-day activities that are saved in a short-term section of the iPhone's memory space known as a cache. Clearing your iPhone cache can release space for storage and, in some instances, velocity it up.

How to Crystal clear the Safari Cache with an iPhone

Probably the most commonly cleared cache on any gadget is the browser cache. That is full of stored images and webpages, cookies, along with other files.

The net browser cache was created to increase your browser by saving files it could need later and that means you don't need to download them again. Clearing Safari's cache might decelerate your browser since it must download formerly cached data. Nevertheless, it's a typical solution once the browser isn't operating properly.

To very clear the cache within Safari:

- Touch the Settings app in the iPhone home display.

- Tap Safari.

- Tap Clear Background and Website Information.

- In the confirmation box, tap Clear History and Data (or tap Cancel if you change your mind).

How to Crystal clear Cache and Short term Files about iPhone

Restarting your iPhone is a superb way to clean its cache. This won't obviously sort every cache: The Safari internet browser cache and some third-party apps will not be cleared, for instance. Still, it is a smart way to delete short-term files to release storage or resolve problems.

How to Crystal clear Cache From Third-Party Apps

on iPhone

Third-party apps that you install in the App Store might or might not enable you to clear their caches. This will depend on whether this is a feature that the developer has put into the app.

The settings to clear caches for a few third-party apps can be found in the iPhone's Settings app. For instance, to apparent the cache from the Accuweather app:

- Touch the iPhone's Settings app.

- Scroll straight down and touch the AccuWeather app.

- Start the Reset cached content material slider.

Clearing the cache in chrome

Occasionally the cache-cleaning configurations are located in the app's configurations, usually in a Configurations menu in the app. The Chromium browser app will be one of these brilliant apps.

158

- Open up the Chrome web browser and touch the three-dot menus icon at the bottom of the display screen.

- Tap Settings.

- Select Privacy.

- Choose Clear Surfing around Data.

Notice: If there is no option to clear the cache in either the app or even the phone's configurations, delete and reinstall the app. This can clear the aged cache and start the app new. Make sure you have adequate knowledge about what you're dropping here, though. You may not need to apparent data for you to carry on.

Reinstall Apps to Crystal clear iPhone Cache

If an app doesn't allow you to clear the cache manually, it is possible to still drive out the app's temporary data files. The solution would be to delete the app from your iPhone and instantly reinstall it.

Head to Settings > Common > iPhone Storage space to find out which apps over the iPhone use up most of the space on your gadget.

Notice: The iPhone Storage space screen lists all of the apps set up on your iPhone and just how much space they use, you start with the ones that use almost all areas.

- In the iPhone Storage display, tap on app.

- Go through the Files & Data collection for that app. This displays how much room the paperwork and data for your app use up on your gadget.

- Once you locate an app you intend to delete, tap Delete app.

When can you clear iphone cache?

The iPhone cache can be an important and useful area of the gadget. It contains documents that you'll require and, in some instances, use up the space on your phone. Having said that, you can find two major factors to clear the iPhone cache.

Firstly, cached files use up storage space on the iPhone, and, as time passes, they accumulate. If you wish to release storage space on your iPhone, clearing the cache will be one method to get it done. Some of that is carried out immediately by iOS, nevertheless, you can also get it done manually.

Another reason to clear the iPhone cache is the fact that cached files sometimes decelerate the working condition (i.e slow down) of the phone.

There are many different varieties of caches in the iPhone. Because of this, there's no solitary step that is possible to take to clear all sorts of the cache.

Ways to Get Tool Into and From iPhone Recovery Setting

If an issue won't resolve with your iOS device, try these pointers. Many issues with the iPhone could be solved by restarting it, however, many more complex issues require placing the iPhone into Recuperation Mode. This must not be your 1st troubleshooting stage, but sometimes it is the only one that works.

What's iPhone Recuperation Mode?

Recovery Mode is a type of last-resort troubleshooting action you can get on an iPhone that's having troubles with its operating-system. Putting a tool into Recovery Setting enables the iPhone to perform and hook up to iTunes, without totally booting in the iOS. Allowing you up-date the Operating system to a fresh, working edition or restore an operating backup onto these devices. You can make use of it, but as you may think, it's something you merely use when other activities won't work.

When to utilize Recovery Mode

You need to use iPhone Recovery Setting once you:

- Install an iOS upgrade, as well as your device, will get stuck in a continuous restart loop. This occurs when something goes wrong using the revise or whenever your battery is incredibly low through the installation.

- Update the operating-system or restore these devices from backup however the course of action fails and iTunes no more sees these devices when you link it.

- Upgrade from the beta version from the iOS.

- See the Apple company logo or Hook up to iTunes icon onscreen for a couple of minutes without change.

Repair your iPhone by making use of Recovery Mode enables you to either up-date the OS or remove all data on these devices. Ideally, there is a current backup of one's information in iCloud or iTunes. Or even, you may find yourself losing any information added in the middle of your final backup and today.

How to Place an iPhone Inside Recovery Mode

To place an iPhone into a recuperation setting, follow these actions:

- Switch your iPhone off by keeping down the rest/wake switch (at the top part on all the iPhones). Hold before the slider appears at the very top and swipe the slider. In case your cell phone doesn't respond, hold the rest/wake key and the power button together before the screen goes darkish.

- Get yourself a computer with iTunes installed on

it. Ideally, this is the PC you sync with, but any personal computer with iTunes onto it could work. Make sure the iTunes system is not operating.

The steps you follow can be determined by what magic size of the iPhone you might have:

- *iPhone 11 or more:* Plug the syncing wire into the iPhone. Hold down the medial side button when you plug another end from the wire into your personal computer.

- *iPhone 12 collection:* Plug the syncing wire into the iPhone. Hold down the volume Down button when you plug another end from the wire into your personal computer.

- *iPhone 13 collection and earlier:* Plug the syncing wire into the iPhone. Hold down the power button when you plug the wire from another end into your personal computer.

A window arises in iTunes which help you to be able to Update or Restore the telephone. Click Up-date. This tries to solve the issue by upgrading the operating-system and without erasing your computer data.

If Update fails, put your iPhone into recuperation mode again each time you click on Restore.

How to Restore iPhone

If you want to restore your iPhone, it is possible to elect to restore it to its factory condition or from the recent backup of one's data.

Ways to Get Away from iPhone Recuperation Mode

If restoring the iPhone succeeds, your telephone will exit Recuperation Setting when it restarts.

You can even exit Recovery Setting without restoring your phone (in case your gadget was working properly before. Or even, Recovery Mode continues to be your best choice). To achieve that:

166

- Unplug these devices from your USB cable.

- Hold the lower volume button (or Part, based on your design) button before iPhone becomes off, then ignore it.

- Keep it down again before the Apple logo reappears.

- Forget about the button and these devices will start upward.

If Recovery Setting Doesn't Work

If getting your iPhone into Recuperation Setting doesn't solve your trouble, the problem could be much more serious than what you can possibly fix by yourself. If so, you should create an appointment in the Genius Pub of one's nearest Apple Shop to get assistance.

Forgot Your iPhone Passcode? Here's How to Fix It

Can't understand passcode? The iPhone's passcode function is an essential way to maintain prying eyes from personal information, but imagine if you forgot your iPhone passcode?

If you forget your passcode and get into the incorrect one on six occasions, your iPhone will let you know it's been disabled. And, based on your configurations, entering the incorrect passcode way too many times may lead to your iPhone deleting most of its information. You don't need that!

Whether you have this message or simply find out you've forgotten your iPhone passcode, follow these actions to regain access to your iPhone.

Repair a Forgotten Passcode By Erasing Your iPhone

There's only one way to correct it once you forget your iPhone passcode. You may not like it, but you need to erase all of the data on your iPhone and restore your computer data from back-up (that's if you do a backup).

Erasing all data from your iPhone also erases the passcode which you forgot and enables you to set up the phone again with a fresh passcode. It may look extreme, nonetheless, it makes sense from the security perspective.

The problem, needless to say, is that approach erases all the data on your iPhone. This is not a problem when you have a recent back-up of that information to restore on your mobile phone (this can be a good reminder: create normal backups of the info on your iPhone!).

The 3 Ways to repair a Forgotten iPhone Passcode

There are 3 ways it is possible to erase the info from your iPhone, take away the passcode, and start new: using iTunes, iCloud, or Recovery Mode.

iTunes: When you have access to your iPhone, sync this regularly having a PC, and also have that PC nearby, this can be the easiest choice. Get step-by-step guidelines on how to effectively make use of iTunes to erase and restore your iPhone on How to Restore Your iPhone From the Backup.

iCloud: If you have enabled Get My iPhone on your device, you should use iCloud to erase it. Utilize this option unless you have access to the phone or if you sync your mobile phone with iCloud rather than iTunes. Have a look at these instructions on how best to make use of iCloud to remove your iPhone.

Recovery Setting: That is your only choice if you've in no way synced your cell phone with iTunes or iCloud. If so, you certainly won't have your computer data backed up and can lose what's on your phone. That isn't good, but at the very least you can use your telephone again. Go through this to understand how to place your iPhone into Recuperation Mode.

How to proceed After Erasing Your iPhone

Whichever of the above options you utilize, you'll end up getting an iPhone that's in Hawaii just as when you initially took it from the box. You have three choices for your next stage:

- **Establishing iPhone from scrape:** Select this if you wish to start completely fresh together with your iPhone and do not want to bring back any data (or haven't any to revive).

- Repairing from backup: That is best when you have a backup of your data, either on iTunes or iCloud, and desire to put it back again on your mobile phone.

- Redownloading content material: Even though you didn't have a backup, virtually anything you've purchased from the iTunes, App, and Apple Books

171

Shops could be redownloaded for your device. Learn to redownload iPhone buys.

Then, set up a fresh passcode on your iPhone-and make sure it's one that is possible to remember!

Imagine If You Forgot a Restrictions or Screen Period Passcode?

There's an added sort of passcode you might have on your iOS device: the passcode that safeguards Limitations or Screen Period.

This passcode allows parents or IT administrators to block certain apps or features and prevents anyone who doesn't know the passcode from changing those settings. But imagine if you're the mother or father or administrator and you also forget your passcode?

If so, the options pointed out previously for erasing and rebuilding from backup will continue to work. Unless you wish to accomplish that, you can find third-party programs that will help you bypass this passcode and regain access to your gadget. We haven't examined every one of the options on the market, so some study at your preferred internet search engine is your greatest bet for getting a tool that will help.

The Bottom Collection About Forgetting an iPhone Passcode

The iPhone's passcode feature being strong is good for security, but bad if you forget your passcode. Don't allow an overlooked passcode now cease you from utilizing a passcode in the foreseeable future; it's too vital for your security. Just ensure that next time you utilize a passcode that'll be easier for you to keep in mind (however, not too an easy task to guess!)

How to Restore Your iPhone From the Backup

The data on your iPhone could be dropped or damaged often: from the repair that required the info to be erased, an accidental deletion, or if files were corrupted. Once you shed your iPhone information, restoring the iPhone from the backup is a basic task that may have your cell phone ready to go very quickly.

How you restore your phone depends on whether you backup your iPhone to iCloud or to iTunes on your PC.

How to Restore iPhone Utilizing an iCloud Backup

In case your iPhone automatically backs up on iCloud once the iPhone is linked to power and Wi-Fi, repairing it is quick and wireless. Before you start the process, ensure that there is a back-up in iCloud.

How To Look For A Good iCloud Backup Around The

174

Iphone

To be sure you've got a recent backup:

- Tap Settings and enter your name.

- Tap iCloud.

- Select Manage Storage space.

- Tap Backups.

- In the Backups section, tap the iPhone entry to show the date and size from the backup.

When there is zero entry or it is a vintage backup, you might have back-up the iPhone to iTunes on the computer sooner or later.

How To Restore A Good Icloud Backup Within The Iphone

After you concur that you've got a usable backup stored iCloud:

- Get back to the primary Settings screen.

175

- Tap General.

- Scroll under and faucet Reset.

- Faucet Erase All Content material and Settings.

- Confirm and touch Erase Now.

- Enter your passcode when prompted.

- Touch Erase iPhone and confirm.

- Enter Your Apple ID security password and faucet Erase.

- The Apple logo design and an improvement pub appear on the display screen. Await for the improvement bar to perform.

- Once the iPhone restarts, register to iCloud together with your Apple ID.

- In the Apps & Data display, tap Recover from iCloud Backup.

- Decide on a backup document from the listing.

176

- Adhere to the on-screen guidelines to perform the Restore course of action.

How to Restore a good iPhone Back-up From iTunes on your PC

Once you sync your iPhone with iTunes on the computer, the info, settings, are supported. To revive a backup for the iPhone:

- Open iTunes using the PC that you use to regress to something easier on the iPhone.

- Link the iPhone to the computer utilizing a USB cable.

- Click on the iPhone symbol to open up the iPhone Summary display screen.

- In the Backups section, click Bring back Backup.

- Choose the backup you intend to use through the list iTunes provides - this may only become one choice - and click on Restore.

177

Enter your Apple company ID information, to start with the backup repair. This is the same account that you set up once you triggered your iPhone at first.

iTunes reloads the back-up data on your phone. The procedure is relatively fast because it just transfers information and settings at this time, not your songs, apps, and pictures. Then, the procedure of downloading your bought music, films, apps, publications, and photos starts, which can have a long time with regards to the number of guides on the iPhone.

How to Repair a good iPhone Stuck around the Apple Logo design

In case your iPhone is stuck in the Apple logo during startup and can not load the home screen at night, it may seem your iPhone is permanently broken. But that could not function as the case may be. Below are a few methods of getting your iPhone from the startup loop and operating properly again.

What Can Cause an iPhone Stuck for the Apple Logo

The iPhone gets stuck in the Apple logo design screen when there is a problem with the operating system or the phone's hardware. It's difficult for the common user to identify the reason behind the issue, but there are many things that leads to this:

- Issues when upgrading to a fresh edition of iOS.

- Issues with jailbreaking the telephone.

- Owning a beta version of iOS which has expired.

- When transferring information from an old device to a fresh one.

- Hardware harm to the internals of the telephone.

How to Repair a good iPhone Stuck over the Apple Logo

In case your iPhone continues to be stuck around the Apple logo display screen for a long period (think 20-30 moments or longer) as well as the improvement bar hasn't changed, you can find three basic steps you should attempt to repair it.

Notice: If these troubleshooting tips don't function, you will have to get in touch with Apple customer support, or visit a good Apple Shop for in-person assistance.

Restart the iPhone. Numerous problems, which include an iPhone trapped on the Apple company logo, could be set with a straightforward restart. Truthfully, a simple restart is not likely to solve the issue in cases like this, but it may be the simplest repair and that means it is worth attempting. It will only cost you a couple of seconds of your energy.

Note: In case a regular restart fails, it's also advisable to get one of these hard reset. A difficult reset clears out more of the iPhone's storage (without the data reduction) and may sometimes fix more challenging problems.

Place the iPhone into Recovery Mode. Recuperation Mode is a particular troubleshooting mode that will help in cases like this. Whenever your iPhone is stuck in the Apple company logo, this means that the operating system is having difficulty starting up. Recuperation Mode shoes up the telephone but halts the Operating system from running to repair it. When using Recuperation Mode, it is possible to install a new edition of iOS or perhaps a backup of one's data. It is a fairly simple process and solves the issue in some instances.

Use DFU Setting. DFU (Gadget Firmware Revise) Mode prevents your iPhone from partway with the startup procedure and lets you restore the iPhone, weight a back-up, or start new. It's much like Recovery Setting, but more centered on solving the type of low-level conditions that trigger the iPhone to be stuck in the Apple company logo. Making use of DFU Mode requires some practice since it requires an exact set of activities, but it is frequently effective.

Get Help From Apple

If you tried all of the above ways and your iPhone continues to stuck in the Apple logo design, it is time to consult professionals. Schedule an appointment with your closest Apple company Store to obtain in-person assistance or contact Apple company Support online.

My iPhone Won't Charge! What Do I Do?

In case your iPhone won't charge, it might be time for a fresh battery (and, because the iPhone's battery can not be changed by an average individual, you'll be spending money on that service combined with the battery itself).

Before you decide to pay to displace your iPhone battery, try the troubleshooting steps out of this guide. There are a variety of other aspects that hinder your iPhone's capability to cost its battery. You might be able to repair the problem yourself and cut costs.

01 Restart iPhone

Restarting your iPhone solves many basic problems people experience today making use of their devices. The procedure won't solve much serious glitches, if a cell phone won't charge, try to restart it and attempt plugging it in once again.

02 Replace USB Cable

There may be an issue using the USB cable you're using for connecting the iPhone to your personal computer or energy adapter. One good option may be the iXCC Element Collection USB wire, which is at 3 feet long, is licensed by Apple company, and works with the iPhone 5 and increased. As an added bonus also, it possesses an

18-month warranty.

03 Replace Walls Charger

If you are charging your iPhone utilizing a walls charger strength adapter instead of plugging it into your personal computer, maybe it's the adapter that's preventing your iPhone from charging.

Just like the USB wire, the only path to check on is simply by getting another power adapter and attempting to charge your phone from it (alternatively, you might try charging utilizing a computer rather).

04 Examine USB Port

You will need a USB 2.0 slot to charge your iPhone. It's likely that that's what you're plugging into, nonetheless it doesn't harm to check.

Knowing that you're using the right type of USB slot, if you nevertheless can't get yourself a charger, it might be the USB interface itself that's broken. To check it, try to plug your iPhone in another USB port on your PC. If that slot recognizes and charges your iPhone, the USB interface on your PC may be damaged.

You can even try plugging in another USB gadget you know for sure works.

05 Don't Charge Using the Keyboard

To be sure that your iPhone charge properly, you will need to be sure you're charging it in the proper place. As the iPhone offers high power needs, it needs to be charged making use of high-speed USB slots. The USB slots that are incorporated on some keyboards don't offer enough capacity to recharge the iPhone.

So, in case your iPhone doesn't appear to be getting a

charge, make sure it's plugged straight into your computer's USB slots, not the keypad or any other peripheral gadget.

06 Make use of iPhone Recuperation Mode

Sometimes issues with your iPhone require a lot more extensive steps to resolve them. One particular measure are Recuperation Mode. That is just like a restart but might help solve more technical problems. In Recuperation Setting, you delete the info on your cell phone. By using Recovery Setting, your telephone will have much of its information restored from the backup or bring it back to factory configurations.

07 Look For Lint

This isn't a typical problem, but it is possible that lint from your pockets or purse could be jammed into the iPhone's Lightning connector. If there's plenty of lint there, it might prevent the phone from connecting correctly and thus stop the iPhone batteryfrom been charge. Check your wire and dock connection for gunk. If you discover it, a goof compressed airflow is the perfect way too but blowing may also work.

08 There is a Dead Battery

If none of the solutions function, it's likely your iPhone's battery is dead and must be replaced. Apple company costs $79 plus shipping and delivery for the support. Spending a while at search engines will bring other companies offering the same services for much less. It's worth keeping in mind, too, that when your iPhone will be less than twelve months old, or when you have AppleCare, electric battery replacement is protected for free.

Chapter 7

4 Methods To Solve Issues With iTunes Buys

Buying a track, book, or movie from the iTunes Store is usually simple and worry-free, but sometimes there are issues with your iTunes buys.

Problems happen for many reasons, but if you lose your web connection through the purchase or download, or there's one on Apple's part, you can finish up spending money on something however, not having the ability to download or play it. A number of the common issues that happen in these circumstances include:

- iTunes says that it's bought but it cannot be downloaded.

- A partly downloaded document that cannot be

performed or used.

- Your credit cards are charged, nevertheless, you can't download.

- A document that seems to have completely downloaded, but doesn't play.

- A failed purchase.

If you are facing one of the above listed problems, here are 4 actions you can take to get this content you payed for from iTunes.

1. How To Proceed If iTunes Purchase Didn't Happen

The easiest kind of iTunes purchase problem to resolve is if the transaction simply wasn't completed. If so, you merely need to choose the item again. You can examine to ensure the purchase didn't happen using iTunes by pursuing these steps:

- Open iTunes.

- Click the Accounts menu.

- Click View My Accounts.

- If you are asked to get your Apple ID accounts, do this and click *Register.*

- Scroll right down to the Purchase Background section.

- Click See All.

- Here, you can see whenever your latest purchase was and what it was. If that you just attempted to buy isn't outlined, your purchase failed and you will need to try again.

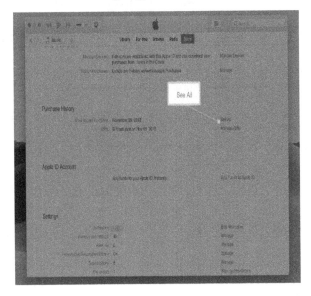

You can even check your purchases using the iTunes Store or App Store applications with an iOS device:

- Touch the application for the type of purchase you're looking at, either iTunes Store or App Store.

- In the App Store, touch your profile icon in the top right, then Purchased.

- Next, faucet My Purchases. When you have Family Posting set up, touch on the average person relative whose buys you want to check on.

- You are able to tap Not upon this iPhone near the top of the app. This shows purchases not presently installed on your device.

- In the iTunes Store app, faucet the More tabs in the bottom, then Purchased. Touch Music, Films, or Television Shows to start to see the item you bought. When you have Family Writing, you can touch the individuals in your loved one's group below.

In both cases, if what you wanted to buy isn't listed, you weren't charged for this and the purchase didn't happen. Just return to the iTunes or App Store and purchase it as if you normally would.

2. Look for Available Downloads in iTunes

In some instances, you may come across a download that starts and then stalls out before it completes. If that's the problem you're facing, you ought to be in a position to restart the download easily by following these steps:

- Open iTunes.

- Click the Accounts menu.

- Click Look for Available Downloads.

- If you are asked to enter your Apple ID, achieve this, then click Check.

- When you have a purchase that didn't download whatsoever or was interrupted, it will begin to download.

3. Redownload iTunes Buys Using iCloud

In case your purchase succeeded however the item you are considering doesn't appear when you follow the steps from the last section to check on for downloads, there's a straightforward solution so you can get your missing content: iCloud. Apple stores all your iTunes and App Store buys in your iCloud accounts where you can simply redownload them.

4. Ways to get iTunes Support From Apple

The first three options in this specific book should solve most iTunes purchase problems. However, if you are one of the unlucky few who's still got a problem even after attempting them, you have two options:

- Get active support from Apple's iTunes support team. For step-by-step instructions about how to achieve that, read this book on requesting support from the iTunes Store.

- Use Apple's online help site to look for the best kind of support for you. This web site will ask you some questions about your problem and, predicated on your answers, offer an article to learn, a person to speak to, or lots to call.

What to do When iTunes Isn't Recognizing Your Iphone

Once you can't play your favorite songs, these solutions

might help. iTunes is Apple's amusement hub, storing all of your songs, movies, Television shows, and much more. To take pleasure from iTunes across all of your devices, Apple enables you to sync iTunes on your PC and iPhone utilizing a USB link. While this generally works well, occasionally iTunes doesn't identify your iPhone, which may be frustrating and complicated.

Take a look at why this issue may occur and how exactly to repair it and get iPhone and iTunes in sync again.

Notice: With macOS Catalina, Apple company Music changed iTunes. These troubleshooting methods apply to techniques with old iTunes versions in addition to newer techniques with Apple Songs.

Factors behind iTunes Not Recognizing iPhone

There are many explanations why iTunes doesn't recognize an iPhone. There could be a physical problem, like a faulty USB wire or USB slot using the PC.

Particles may clog the iPhone interface, or there may be a software issue.

Whatever the way may be to solve the issue, there are a few quick troubleshooting steps with a higher potential for getting an iPhone and iTunes back again.

How to correct it when itunes won't recognize your iphone

Often, iPhone-to-iTunes connectivity problems stem from issues it is possible to fix. Attempt each troubleshooting phase to find out if it solves the issue. If it generally does not, move on to another suggestion.

Make sure iTunes is set up using the PC. Unless you have iTunes, this program can't understand the device. You can set up iTunes (or its successor, Apple company Music) on the Mac or Home windows PC.

Examine the USB wire. A faulty USB wire might lead to the iPhone-to-iTunes link issue. Make sure the USB wire is in good condition. Whether it's frayed or slice, use various USB cable and find out if this solves the issue.

Verify the iPhone's slot. Sometimes, debris accumulation leads to an iPhone interface to fail. Work with a dried out, anti-static clean or toothbrush to completely clean it out softly. Then, connect once again and find out if this fixes the problem.

Check out the USB slot using the PC. Start by unplugging all USB products from the PC. Proceed to the iPhone's wire to another interface and reconnect. If this functions, there's a problem with the specific port, and you will need to repair.

Restart the iPhone. A little software glitch might lead to a faulty link. Restart these devices and connect once again.

Restart the computer. A moderate software insect or breakdown could cause iTunes to breakdown. Switch off the PC and leave it for a couple of minutes before switching it back on again.

Make sure the iOS device is be unlocked and on the home screen. Connect these devices, instantly unlock it, and make sure it's on the home screen. Then link your iPhone to iTunes.

Download the most recent edition of iTunes. A vintage edition of iTunes might not acknowledge your iPhone. Upgrade iTunes and attempt to link the iPhone once again.

Update operating-system software. Update Home windows or macOS and find out if this manages any software program glitches or concealed bugs that triggered the iPhone-to-iTunes link problem.

Check the machine Report. This just applies if you are using a Mac PC. Connect the iPhone and check out the System Statement, which shows energetic devices. In case your iPhone is displayed, nevertheless, you can't link, you may be experiencing a software program issue.

Disable or uninstall security software. If you are using a Mac as well as the iPhone have been listed in the machine Record, disable or uninstall antivirus software program and other protection programs individually. Find out if any system causes the issue.

Reinstall the Apple company Mobile Gadget USB driver. This driver informs the PC how to proceed with Apple gadgets. When it malfunctions, it generally does not read the gadget properly. Reinstall the car owner and find out if this solves the issue.

Uninstall and reinstall iTunes. A breakdown of iTunes can often be solved by uninstalling and reinstalling the program.

Get in touch with Apple Help. The Apple company iTunes assistance website offers numerous helpful features, which includes a searchable understanding base and the capability to ask the city a question. You can even set up a scheduled appointment on the Genius Club of your nearby Apple Store.

How to Backup on iPhone Without iTunes

For quite some time, you had to use iTunes to backup your iPhone. But you start with macOS Catalina (15), iTunes no more exists. Just how do you regress to something easier on your iPhone? There are variety of choices on how to backup your iPhone online without iTunes.

How to Support iPhone in macOS Catalina

Since iTunes was retired, you start with macOS Catalina (15), you may expect that Apple company Music, this program that replaced it, is where you back up your iPhone. That's affordable, but it isn't right. Rather, in macOS Catalina, you support your iPhone in the Finder. Some tips about what to accomplish:

- Link your iPhone to your Mac utilizing a USB wire and unlock the phone.

- Open a fresh Finder window.

- In the left-hand sidebar from the Finder window, click your iPhone. Unless you see it, increase the Locations area.

- The iPhone administration screen appears in the Finder window. This display allows you to handle the sync and backup configurations for your cell phone. In Backups, click on Back up all the data on your own iPhone to the Mac.

How to Backup iPhone Files Online Making use of iCloud

Another solution to online backup of your iPhone without iTunes is by using iCloud. With iCloud, all your backups are usually wireless and may be done immediately whenever your iPhone is locked, linked to Wi-Fi, and connected to a power resource. Here's how to set up your iPhone to back up on iCloud:

- Make sure you're signed in to the iCloud account on your iPhone.

- Link your iPhone to Wi-Fi.

- Tap Settings.

- Near the top of the Settings display screen, tap your title.

- Tap iCloud.

- Tap iCloud Back-up.

- Turn the iCloud Backup slider to on/natural.

- You're done. Your iPhone is defined to automatically back up its information to iCloud whenever it's secured, linked to Wi-Fi, and connected to strength.

How to Backup iPhone Making use of Third-Party Programs

Are you not thinking for a better ways of using the Finder or iCloud for the iPhone backups without iTunes? You can find third-party programs you can make use of. These paid applications support your iPhone to some Mac or PC. They also frequently add additional functions that other back-up options don't possess, such as permitting you to recover deleted data files or access concealed files. Remember, it's not necessary that the Finder and iCloud back-up are the only good options (and already incorporated with your Macintosh).

There are a large number of third-party iPhone backup programs and we haven't reviewed all of them, so we don't have a recommendation for you to use.

Chapter 8

How To Use iCloud Keychain To Control And Store Your Passwords

While security password managers have long existed as third-party applications on iOS and macOS, Apple has doubled down alone attempts. iCloud Keychain is an attribute on macOS and iOS that stores passwords, credit cards information, and more.

iCloud Keychain's been around for quite some time, but it continues to obtain additional powerful and able with each era of iOS and macOS. For example, iOS 14 and macOS Mojave added new features that automatically create strong and unique passwords for every website and application you utilize. This security password is automatically stored in iCloud Keychain and easy to get at from all your devices.

iCloud Keychain remembers things so you don't have to. It auto-fills your details - like your Safari usernames and passwords, bank cards, Wi-Fi passwords, and interpersonal log-ins - on any device that you approve.

How to Setup iCloud Keychain

The very first thing you'll wish to accomplish is to make sure you've created two-factor authentication. This makes iCloud Keychain much simpler to use across all your devices.

Once you've done that, on your Mac you'll want to open up the machine Preferences application and go directly to the iCloud app. For the reason that list, you should see "Keychain," where you can tick the checkbox to allow it.

On iOS, open up the Settings app, faucet your name at the very top, then touch "iCloud." Scroll through the set of applications using iCloud to check out "Keychain." Faucet it and ensure that it's toggled toward "On."

How to gain access to iCloud Keychain passwords

Much like any password supervisor, a very important factor you'll want to ensure is that you always learn how to gain access to the passwords and data stored in iCloud Keychain.

On iOS:

- Open Settings
- Scroll right down to "Passwords & Accounts"
- Touch "Website & App Passwords"

- Authenticate via Face ID or Touch ID

On Mac pc:

- Open Safari

- In the menu pub, click "Safari" then "Choices"

- Search for "Passwords" along the very best

Now you'll visit a clear set of passwords and login information for each website. Apple will also warn you if you've reused the same security password on multiple websites, and offer a quick connect to change your security password on the service's website.

You can even copy and paste usernames and passwords, and Airdrop these to other devices.

On macOS and iOS, iCloud Keychain will show itself at nearly every login screen, letting you easily gain access to your account. It will offer autofill recommendations for card obligations, your address, and more.

iCloud Keychain can be an incredibly powerful way to

control your passwords, credit card details, and more, with the necessity for a third-party app.

How to Unlock iCloud-Locked iPhones

Getting an iPhone that has an iCloud lock is a problem as you can't utilize the phone and unless you unlock it, and doing this may not be easy. Your very best bet would be to determine what it means with an iCloud-locked iPhone, how to fix this problem, and what to prevent when attempting to open it up once again.

What's an iCloud-Locked iPhone?

iCloud locking is usually Activation Lock, which is a feature Apple company introduced in iOS 15 to avoid iPhone thefts.

Your iPhone or iPad automatically converts on Activation Lock whenever Find My iPhone is dynamic. As soon as you enable the function, no one can delete these devices,

209

activate it on other accounts, or disable Discover My iPhone without getting into the Apple ID account that originally set up the phone.

Activation Lock is an efficient anti-theft gauge. A thief probably won't have the iCloud account for the individual whose mobile phone they stole, and without it, the telephone won't work.

How to Know When a good iPhone Is iCloud Locked

If you notice onscreen information that reads Activation Lock, the telephone is iCloud locked and require the initial Apple ID account you used to create the telephone to unlock it.

Are iCloud-Locked Cell phones Stolen?

Because an iPhone is teaching an Activation Lock information, that doesn't indicate it's stolen. It is possible to allow Activation Lock unintentionally. Some situations where this could occur include:

- Forgetting to carefully turn off Discover My iPhone before erasing the iPhone

- Forgetting to signal from iCloud before erasing the iPhone

- In case your Apple ID is disabled.

In those cases, you'll receive the Activation Lock screen when attempting to set up the telephone again. These errors are somewhat typical when buying used iPhones.

Having said that, iCloud locking can be a sign there could be grounds to suspect the cell phone is stolen. If you are buying a used iPhone, make sure to inquire whether Activation Lock will be disabled, and when it isn't, don't choose the phone.

Note: Whilst they both use the "secured" terminology, a good iCloud-locked phone isn't exactly like a secured phone. "Secured" often means that the telephone requires a passcode to be able to access it. Additionally, it may mean that the telephone is linked with a single cell phone company, usually as long as you're under the agreement. Any phone could be secured to something provider. They have nothing in connection with Activation Lock, iCloud, or stolen phones.

How to Unlock a good iCloud-Locked iPhone

If you start to see the Activation Lock display around the iPhone you're attempting to activate, enter the Apple ID account first used to activate the telephone, and the telephone will open. If you forgot your Apple company ID password, you will have to reset it.

If you're working on iOS 11 or newer version and you use Two-Factor Authentication to secure your Apple ID, it is possible to disable Activation Lock making use of your gadget passcode. Select Unlock with Passcode, faucet Use Gadget Passcode, and enter the passcode.

The procedure gets more technical when the account isn't

yours, like if you bought a used iPhone. If an iPhone is iCloud-locked to a merchant account apart from yours, you've got a few options.

If the individual whose account was originally used is physically in your area:

- Enter their Apple company ID account qualifications on the telephone.

- When the telephone gets to the home screen, they ought to sign away from iCloud:

- On iOS 10.2 and previous, head to Settings > iCloud > Indication Out.

- On iOS 10.3 or more, head to Settings > [your title] > Indication Out.

- When asked for his or her Apple ID account, you need to enter it once again.

Take away the Apple ID from your iPhone:

- On iOS 10.2 and earlier, touch Sign Out there, then faucet Delete from My iPhone.

- On iOS 10.3 or more, tap Switch Off.

- Erase the telephone again by visiting Settings > Total > Reset > Erase All Content material and Settings.

When the mobile phone restarts this time around, you shouldn't start to see the Activation Lock display screen.

That's the simple version. The somewhat harder version arrives when the individual whose account you will need isn't actually near you. If so, they have to take away the lock making use of iCloud, using this method:

- Keep these things head to iCloud.com and register with their Apple company ID.

- Select Get iPhone.

- Select All Products, then choose the iPhone that should be unlocked.

214

- Select Erase and follow any on-screen prompts.

After the previous owner has removed the phone using their accounts, restart the iPhone, and you won't see the Activation Lock display when it starts.

If You Cannot Get the Initial Account Used to Activate the telephone

Unless you have ways to log in using the iPhone's original accounts, you're stuck. Activation Lock is a powerful and efficient tool and you also can't bypass it. It is critical to make sure used phones aren't iCloud-locked before you get them.

One of the option you need would be to get in touch with Apple. When you can supply valid proof of purchase to Apple company, the company might be ready to unlock the telephone for you. Get yourself a receipt or additional proof of purchase, and then get in touch with Apple for technical support to find out if indeed they can help.

About Sites Promising to iCloud Unlock My Phone

If you have done any Googling on this subject, you tend to have likely run into dozens of websites and forum articles fom various blogs claiming others may bypass iCloud hair. Some may contact themselves "recognized" unlocks. Whatever the state, they're all frauds seeking to get cash for something they can't offer. The only thing around an iCloud lock may be the initial Apple ID utilized to activate the telephone.

These solutions claiming to bypass iCloud hair are usually either just seeking to take your cash, or they might be engaged in a more complicated fraud scheme.

Note: Several services will get around Activation Lock, however in doing this, they crack your phone's link with Apple. You will not have the ability to up-date the operating-system or activate the telephone once again after erasing its information, among other restrictions.

Those are very big drawbacks, and it's really hard to observe how they're worthwhile.

Chapter 9

How to Make use of AssistiveTouch on your iPhone

Including an onscreen home button for your, iPhone could be great. It's your very best bet for keeping your iPhone operating if it includes a damaged home button. It is also crucial for those who have accessibility difficulties. And, it's an excellent shortcut for some helpful features. To include a Home switch, use a function known as AssistiveTouch on iPhone.

What's AssistiveTouch?

AssistiveTouch places a virtual home button on your iPhone's display. This virtual home button lets you perform the same activities as pressing the home key, but by tapping an onscreen image instead. Also, it contains shortcuts to typical tasks that include the Home switch and lets you customize the shortcuts set off by tapping it.

AssistiveTouch was created for people who have physical conditions which makes it hard to allow them to push the button. Since that time, it has been used as a workaround for damaged Home control keys (for example, it can help repair an iPhone that will not switch off), by people who are concerned that the Home key will degrade if they click on it in an excessive way (that isn't true, incidentally), and by those that like the capability of the feature.

How to Place a Home Switch on your iPhone Display With AssistiveTouch

To add a home button for your iPhone screen simply by enabling AssistiveTouch, follow these measures:

- In iOS 13 or more tap Settings > Accessibility.

- If you are using iOS 12, head to Settings > General > Accessibility.

- Go to Contact > AssistiveTouch to get the button to carefully turn it on.

- If you are using iOS 12, simply tap AssistiveTouch through the Accessibility screen.

- On the AssistiveTouch screen, shift the slider to on/green.

- A new, icon, appears on your screen. That's your brand-new virtual onscreen home button.

How to Make use of AssistiveTouch on iPhone

With AssistiveTouch touch fired up, here's how exactly to use it.

Tapping the icon introduces a menu with the next options:

Notifications: Provides fast access to Notification.

Custom: Enables you to access any custom made shortcuts or activities you've created.

Device: Gives one-touch access to normal features that include locking the telephone, raising and decreasing volume, mute, and much more.

Siri: Launches Siri (big shock, right?).

Control Middle: Reveals Handle Middle (another surprise).

Home: The same as clicking the home button. Similar to the bodily Home button, you can even double-tap it.

Once you select these options, it is possible to return by tapping the trunk arrow at the biggest market of the window.

You pull and fall the AssistiveTouch symbol to move around the display screen to a posture that's preferred or beneficial to you.

How to Customize AssistiveTouch in iPhone

Want to modify the actions which are triggered once you touch or double faucet the AssistiveTouch on-screen home button? It is possible to. Just adhere to these tips:

- In iOS 13 or more, head to Settings > Accessibility > Contact > AssistiveTouch.

- In iOS 12, head to Settings > Common > Convenience > AssistiveTouch.

It is possible to control what goes on to get a Single-Tap, Double-Tap, or even Long Press. Touch the menu at the action you intend to customize.

Select the actions you want in the available list.

For Double-Tap and Long Press, you can even control the number of times necessary for the actions before it's time out. Handle this in the Double-Tap Timeout and Long Push Duration selections, respectively.

How to Switch Off AssistiveTouch about iPhone

Don't need your onscreen home button anymore? Switch off AssistiveTouch by following these actions:

- In iOS 13 or more, tap Settings > Accessibility > Contact > AssistiveTouch.

- If you are using iOS 12, head to Settings > General > Accessibility > AssistiveTouch.

- Proceed the AssistiveTouch slider to off/white.

How to Make use of Voice Memos on iPhone

Apple's Tone of voice Memos is a free of charge app that enables you to record sound on iPhone, iPad, and Apple Watch. This tone of voice recorder application includes an easy streamlined style with a basic report and edit features, it also help with the capability to export audio recordings to some other services for back-up, sharing, or even more advanced editing.

Notice: The Tone of voice Memos app arrives to set up on all iOS products, but if you've erased it, it is possible to reinstall it from your App Store free of charge.

How to Report on iPhone Using the Tone of voice Memos App

Recording audio using the iPhone Tone of voice Memos app is quite easy. Here's how to record tone of voice on iPhone.

- Open the Tone of voice Memos app on your iPhone or any iOS device.

- Touch the red report button at the bottom of the display to start voice recording afresh.

Note: Only a fast tap is okay. You don't have to hold it.

- Tap the tiny red horizontal collection for you to view more options regarding your document. In the display screen that opens, it is possible to pause the recording and continue it to help keep several recordings in the same sound file.

- Touch the red quit button when you wish to stop documenting.

- Select New record near the top of the display and type a name for that record. The record is saved beneath the name you type.

How to Cut a Tone of voice Memo in iPhone

Apple's Tone of voice Memos app includes just basic editing efficiency. Here's how to cut a voice recording in the app.

- Touch the audio record you intend to edit on the Voice Memos starting screen.

- Touch the ellipsis.

- Tap Edit Saving.

- Touch the crop icon.

- Pull the yellow deals at the bottom of the display screen to enclose the portion of the record you intend to keep.

- Tap Trim to eliminate any area of the saving outside the cut handles.

- Tap Save to verify the changes.

- To delete a portion of the sound, faucet the crop symbol, choose an area of the timeline and touch

Delete. Finally, faucet Save.

- When you've finished making all your edits towards the audio file, touch Done.

How to Delete a good iPhone Tone of voice Memo

To delete a voice record in the Tone of voice Memos app, faucet the record, after that tap the garbage to close it.

You won't get a confirmation prompt, but if you accidentally delete a record, you may get it back. Touch the Lately Deleted category, touch the file's title, then faucet Recover > Recover Record.

How to Send Tone of voice Memos on iPhone

Once recorded, audio record in the Tone of voice Memos app could be delivered to a multitude of app.

- Tap the document you intend to send.

- Touch the ellipsis.

- Tap Share.

- Tap a get in touch to deliver it or export it for an app.

You can even scroll right down to backup the Apple Tone of voice Memo record with a cloud storage space service like Dropbox or even tap Save to Files to save lots of it for your device.

Note: If you experience any mistakes when exporting or even burning your recording, try to send it to yourself by an e-mail, open the document on your PC, and send it to your selected service or get in touch with following that.

The tone of voice Memos App Tips

The voice recorder in iPhone app, Tone of voice Memos, could be very helpful tool for conducting interviews or taking notes. You can also use it to record phone calls.

Below are a few useful ideas to get almost all from it.

Examine your storage: While Tone of voice Memos records can technically choose how long it will be, they are limited by the number of free of charge space on your device. If required, you can release some space.

Do a check documenting: Before performing a significant long-form interview, execute a fast 10-second check records to make sure that everything's operating fine in which background noise is completely filter.

Use a mic: You don't have to work with a mic, but linking someone to your iPhone may greatly enhance audio quality. Remember that you might need a dongle.

Backup your records instantly: Like a precaution, it's a good concept to e-mail yourself a duplicate of the tone of voice recording when it's done or back it up to cloud support like OneDrive or Search engines Drive. In this manner, your essential audio won't be lost if you lose or crack your iPhone.

Chapter 10

How to Opt directly into Contact Tracing on iPhone

Using the growing dependence on the use of a contact tracing app wherever you're on the planet, it is critical to learn how to opt directly into contact tracing on your cellphone in addition to how to opt-out if you choose against taking part in the procedure.

Note: Around this composing, contact tracing can only be enabled on your iPhone when you have download the compatible get in touch with tracing app for your device. Just a handful of says currently have accessible get in touch with tracing apps offered.

Here's how to opt-in addition to opt from getting in touch with tracing on the iPhone.

Note: These details primarily pertain to mobile phone get in touch with tracing within the united states but a lot of the info is pertinent for other nations that are furthermore adopting get in touch with tracing apps.

Preparing Your Telephone for getting in touch with Tracing

Due to how iPhones function, you must have your iOS gadget with iOS 13.5 or above to trigger cellphone get in touch with tracing. That's as the procedure Bluetooth uses to get in touch with tracing strategies that need an update to operate across all smartphones.

You also have to use a health tracking app that works in the contact tracing effort. In America, your decision to use publicity notifications is manufactured by each state's general public health authority therefore different states

231

have gotten different apps and some are choosing never to offer this type of service. It is critical to install the proper app for the state.

How to Opt-In to get hold of Tracing about iPhone

In America, you must opt-in to participate any COVID-19 based smartphone contact tracing. That's furthermore the case far away like the UK, so it is important to learn how to opt into the service on your iPhone. Apple identifies it as Publicity Notifications but it is the ditto as getting in touch with tracing. Some tips about what to do to obtain all initiated.

Be aware: *To activate Direct exposure to Notifications/COVID-19 get in touch with tracing, you will need to install the most recent iOS revise-13.5 or above-as well as possess a related health monitoring app installed.*

- On your iPhone, tap Settings.

- Scroll straight down and tap Personal privacy.

- Tap Health.

- Tap COVID-19 Publicity Logging.

- Tap Direct exposure Logging to toggle the environment on.

Take note: *If establishing this isn't accessible to you in your area or you do not have a relevant wellness tracking app set up.*

You've right now opted-in to COVID-19 Exposure Logging and contact tracing. The general public health app you might have set up will now monitor any moment you're subjected to COVID-19.

How to Opt-out from Contact Tracing in iPhone

In America, you must select to opt into the contact tracing app plan for the data to be shared anonymously with others. That's furthermore the case in lots of other countries. Nevertheless, if you've selected to opt-in after that at a later time changed your mind, how will you opt-out? Here's how to opt-out contact tracing in a few easy steps.

- On your iPhone, tap Settings.

- Scroll lower and tap Personal privacy.

- Tap Health.

- Tap COVID-19 Publicity Logging.

- Tap Direct exposure Logging to toggle the leaving.

Notice: If this placing isn't accessible to you, that's because you no longer possess a relevant wellness tracking app set up. It's been instantly switched off.

You'll no more share your direct exposure information with others anonymously.

How to Delete Publicity Logs

Get in touch with tracing also creates some logs that

bargain of all requests to check on your exposure sign in the last 2 weeks. It is possible to remove these without choosing from the get in touch with tracing effort. Here's how to do it.

- On your iPhone, tap Settings.

- Scroll straight down and tap Personal privacy.

- Tap Health.

- Tap COVID-19 Direct exposure Logging.

- Tap Delete Publicity Log.

- Your records are deleted.

Chapter 11

How to Develop a 'Hey Siri Shortcut for iPhone

The Shortcuts feature in iOS automates both fundamental and complex tasks to save lots of time and help to make your phone usage better. Along with producing your personal 'Hey Siri, I'm obtaining drawn over' shortcuts, it is possible to download ready-made shortcuts from the web.

One pre-programmed shortcut shows up thanks to Robert Petersen, who created it to greatly help people protect themselves during encounters with the authorities. Here are what it can and ways to get it.

What Will the 'I'm Finding Pulled Over' Shortcut Carry out?

As soon as you activate this shortcut, your cell phone performs the next actions:

- Activates Usually Do Not Disturb, which converts off all notifications for inbound calls and communications.

- Sets the display brightness to no.

- Sends a text to some selected connection with where you are in Apple company Maps.

- Starts recording the video from your front (selfie) digital camera.

After you quit documenting, your phone will:

- Turn off Usually Do Not Disturb.

- Save the movie in your Recent folder in Photos and deliver a copy to the recipients you designate.

- Prompt you to upload the movie to iCloud Generate or Dropbox.

Ways to get the 'I'm Getting Drawn More than' Shortcut

Before you use Petersen's plan, you need to inform your iPhone to permit "untrusted" shortcuts. These macros are usually ones that you will get from the web instead of in the Shortcuts app. To regulate this setting, open up the Configurations app, go for Shortcuts, and tap the change close to Allow Untrusted Shortcuts to on/natural.

Now, you're prepared to set up the "I'm Obtaining Stopped" shortcut. Some tips about what to accomplish.:

- Go directly to the Shortcut's guide on Reddit to discover an URL to the most present version.

- Open that hyperlink using Safari on your iPhone.

- Tap Find Shortcut.

- The Shortcuts app will open, and you will see a set of everything it can. Scroll right down to evaluate most of its features.

- At the bottom of the web page, tap Add Untrusted

Shortcut.

- In the next stage, choose more recipients. Individuals you choose right here will receive a copy of the movie you take. It is possible to select the same recipients as in the last action or different styles. Tap Done to complete setting up.

- You'll go back to the Gallery page from the Shortcuts app.

- You might still have to give some permissions before the shortcut will continue to work properly. To start, open the Configurations app.

- Select Shortcuts.

- Tap Location.

- Chose the degree of permission you intend to offer the Shortcuts app. To save lots of time if you are operating on the shortcut, selected With all the App.

- Go back to the Shortcuts app and make sure you're on *My Shortcuts tabs*.

- Tap the greater (three dots) menu in the upper-right part from the I'm obtaining stopped shortcut.

- Scroll right down to Camera and faucet Allow Access.

- Tap OK in the small windows that open.

- Repeat Actions 15 and 16 for Photos and Communications.

- Automagically, this shortcut uses your front-facing camera, nevertheless, you can also select a various one. Tap the Front side under Camera and select Back if you'd like to use some other camera.

- Finally, scroll right down to the Scripting section to select where to upload your video by the end of the shortcut. Automagically, you should use iCloud Push, Dropbox, or perhaps a "Usually do not upload" choice. Touch the minus switch and Delete to eliminate several options.

- Select Done to save lots of your settings.

To run this program, possibly open up the Shortcuts app and touch its button in the *My Shortcuts display screen*, or even activate Siri and state, "I'm getting stopped."

How to Move Songs From iPhone to iPhone

Drifting regularly between 2 iPhones or just desire to send music to some other device, like an adored one's iPhone? You can find multiple ways to share songs with some other iPhone that may be complicated when all you have to do will be share some preferred tracks with somebody.

How to Download Songs to iPhone Making use of Apple

Music

If you sign up for Apple Music, it's incredibly easy to download songs to another iPhone or exchange everything via the Apple Music design feature that allows you to utilize Apple Music across several devices via the same account. To take action, you require to carefully turn on Sync Collection to access your songs library. Here's how to set points up.

- On your main iPhone, tap Settings.

- Scroll straight down and tap Songs.

- Tap Sync Collection toggle it about.

Your songs will now sync across to any iPhones which are signed in on a single account. You don't need to do other things for you to start seeing the music.

How to Exchange Songs Between iPhones Making use of Home Sharing

If you wish to talk about songs (or other documents) in the middle of your iPhones and they are all on the same Wi-Fi network, you should use an attribute called Home Sharing to create it probably. It's obtainable through iTunes permitting around five computers in your household in addition to all of your iOS products and Apple Televisions to share content material. This method is usually ideal if you to want to talk about other files such as photos with gadgets such as your home's Apple TV. Here's how to arrange it in the middle of your iPhones making use of your Mac like a go-between.

- On your own Mac, click on the Apple icon.

- Click System Choices.

- Click Sharing.

- Click Media Posting.

- Click Home Revealing.

- Sign in with your Apple ID and click on Turn On Home Sharing.

Now that Home Sharing is turned on across all of your devices on a single Wi-Fi network, it's easy to use on your iPhone. Some tips on what to do.

- On your own iPhone, tap Music.

- Tap Library.

- Tap Home Spreading.

At this point, you have access to the home Sharing Library of music any moment you're linked to the same Wi-Fi network.

How to Move Songs Between iPhones Making use of AirDrop

AirDrop can be an often forgotten basic method of transferring songs between any Mac PC or iOS gadget.

Impressively, it works for moving music, it also requires seconds. Some tips about what to do.

- On the iPhone, tap Music.

- Find the track you intend to transfer.

- Tap the 3 dots icon.

- Tap Share.

- Tap AirDrop.

- Touch the iPhone you intend to deliver it to.

Acknowledgments

The Glory of this book success goes to God Almighty and my beautiful Family, Fans, Readers & well-wishers, Customers and Friends for their endless support and encouragements.

Index

V